Flown the Nest

Flown the Nest

HANNA GREALLY

First published in 2009 by Attic Press
Attic Press is an imprint of Cork University Press
Youngline Industrial Estate
Pouladuff Road, Togher
Cork, Ireland

British Library Cataloguing in Publication Data

Greally, Hanna.
    Flown the nest.
    1. Greally, Hanna.   2. Mentally ill--Rehabilitation--
    Ireland--Longford (County)   3. Irish--England--Biography.
    I. Title
    362.2'1'092-dc22

    ISBN-13: 9781855942127

Printed by ColourBooks Ltd, Ireland
Typeset by Tower Books, Ballincollig, Co. Cork

www.corkuniversitypress.com

Contents

Foreword   7

PART ONE: COOLAMBER MANOR:
THE REHABILITATION STORY

1	Arrival at Coolamber	15
2	Aims and Purposes	17
3	Group A	19
4	The President and Autumn	21
5	Halloween	25
6	Visitors to Coolamber	27
7	Our Progress	29
8	Preparations for Christmas	30
9	Christmas	33
10	A New Term	37
11	A Thousand Chickens Arrive	40
12	Spring at Coolamber	41
13	Mid-term Tests	43

14	Easter Holidays	46
15	Group C and the Notice Board	48
16	The Merry Month of May	50
17	Pakenham Hall	52
18	Summer Days	54
19	Last Days at Coolamber	56
20	Last Words	58

PART TWO: THE HOUSEKEEPER

	Introduction	63
1	My First Job	65
2	The Next Step	68
3	The Emigrant Ship	72
4	The Shagalls	74
5	The Monastery	84
6	Two Interviews	91
7	Dr Silhou	95
8	The Orderly	101
9	A Day Off	104
10	Dr Joseph OBE	108
11	The Milkman and Others	111
12	Two Strange Encounters	116
13	A Sorrowful Ending	121
14	To Joseph	123
15	Last Days in England	125

Foreword

The arrival of Hanna Greally at the door of Coolamber Manor in County Longford in 1962, described with great feeling in the opening paragraphs, is replete with a deep significance to which the author provides no hint. Coolamber Manor was a state-run rehabilition centre, which had just begun providing residential training of young women for employment. Most had physical disabilities. Hanna, unlike them, had come from a psychiatric hospital. Understanding this context is a key to understanding much of Hanna's life and written work.

Her walk across the threshold of Coolamber, in the 'soft, peaty air', were her first steps towards an uncertain freedom following eighteen years as an involuntary inmate of in St Loman's Hospital in nearby Mullingar. Hanna had crossed its threshold in 1943 as a young woman, not yet twenty, for a 'rest' on foot of a civil committal signed by her widowed mother. She did not leave again until a new regime was in place and a new superintendent released her to Coolamber's care. By then she was, in her own words, an 'embarrassing resurrection', a middle-aged woman, 'sadder and wiser' without family, home, place or status.

When Hanna's freedom was finally restored to her it is doubtful that anyone could have anticipated what she would do with her life and abilities, most particularly with her ability to write. For Hanna went on to copiously narrate her life onto paper in a habit which we know began in her teenage years when her poetry was published in her home-town newspaper in Athlone. Now with the publication of *Flown the Nest* by Attic Press, we have a more complete story; as complete, that is, as most thinly disguised autobiographies of hard times, disappointments and small joys can be, for there is a lot that Hanna has left untold and which may never be told.

Bird's Nest Soup, the story of psychiatric incarceration, was published three times since 1971, most recently in 2008. Here, now, we have the sequels: first, *Coolamber Manor*, the story of transition back into society and into independent adulthood, which was previously serialised in a provincial newspaper in 1972; and second, *Housekeeper at Large*, the story of triumph, her account of her life as a woman of (modest) means and autonomy as a housekeeper and cook, published here for the first time. Indeed, it had been assumed that this manuscript was irretrievably lost and its discovery in 2008 was astonishing, not least given the renewed interest in the author arising from the re-publication of *Bird's Nest Soup*.

Hence these two texts belong as part of a piece, alongside the first book, that is a rare account of one Irish woman's life history through forced psychiatric committal, emigration on the former cattle ships to domestic work in Britain, and eventual return, like so many emigrants, to an uncertain future in an Ireland that, by the 1970s, was more open and more optimistic.

In *Housekeeper at Large*, Hanna, as narrator and biographer, muses that she would continue writing about her life, following her return to Ireland. We do not know if she wrote such an account. Given her proclivity and her growing confidence as a writer – evident particularly in these pages – it is possible that a manuscript was begun. We do know that, after the initial flurry of fame and attention from the publication of *Bird's Nest Soup*,

8

Hanna's life was hard, albeit supported by friends and neighbours and suffused, as ever, with a strong sense of her own worth. She lived on her own in rural Roscommon where she bought a small cottage. She wrote poems and stories. She bred dogs somewhat chaotically. In truth, for just a short time perhaps, she achieved the kind of life that she fantasised about in *Housekeeper at Large*: independent, secure and in charge of her own affairs. Ill health – surely not helped by the smoking habit which, like many in psychiatric institutions, she had adopted – cut her life a little short, however, and when she died at the age of sixty-three in 1987, she was poor, dependent on others and her house was neglected. On her death, the green-ribbon typed pages of *Housekeeper at Large*, which were being prepared for publication, seem also to have died. That fate, thankfully, was metaphorical and not literal.

And what of the place of these books now? As with *Bird's Nest Soup*, we have here a combination of autobiographical narrative and social history. This mode of writing constitutes one important feature of the work. The books capture marginalised social worlds written from the inside, from the lives of the largely invisible and unnoticed which are part of our collective history and unconscious. Reading *Housekeeper at Large,* we are reminded, for instance, of the thousands of Irish women, especially those who never married, who became, in practice, housewives without the comforts, securities and intimacies of marriage and family life, its attendant rights and sense of belonging, who like her had left Ireland in search of a place in the world and found it in other people's homes across Britain and the United States. But there is also here a singular voice which is itself compelling. Hanna was a good storyteller with insightful stories to tell.

Readers of these books will find their own meaning and respond in accordance with their own life stories, their family histories, their understanding of Irish society and Irish women's lives, the tales of emigration and return, and tales of lost or never-found loves. One quality which is striking throughout Hanna's work is the complete absence of self-pity and it is what makes her books so intriguing. The defiance and spirit that characterised *Bird's Nest Soup* is found here in these two texts and serves both to create a writing style which strives for humour and vividness over self-preoccupation, and to allow her to write simply about a life which must have been resonant with complex angers and frustrations. She continues, as in *Bird's Nest Soup,* to be an inveterate observer of our human frailties and vanities, and of our need to seek out company, dignity and meaning wherever we find ourselves. These books are all intimate, careful portraits of domestic, hidden spaces and hidden lives.

We can read *Coolamber Manor* as a book of passage, detailing how Hanna threw herself wholeheartedly into what was akin to a second chance to grow from dependency (institutional rather than familial) to independence. If *Bird's Nest Soup* was dark, raw and powerful, then *Coolamber Manor* abandons that rawness for something more measured but not yet fully mature. *Housekeeper at Large* represents a stylised, comedic attempt to write with a fully adult voice that is controlled and a little distant, though moving closer to the literary. Readers can appreciate a writer learning the craft of writing, drawing endlessly on her own constrained, quotidian life as raw material.

Undoubtedly, Hanna had ability. We do not know how much tutoring she got but *Housekeeper at Large*, her most mature work, is as neat and brassy as the Galway gynaecologist's plaque that she polished every morning as a dutiful, if unconvinced, housekeeper.

It is inevitable, given the St Loman's experience, that we might peruse these works for evidence of trauma, loss or an institutionalised mind. And, between the lines most especially, such is plentiful. In *Coolamber Manor* Hanna inhabits the same kind of tightly supervised, closed space with her fellow trainees that characterised confinement in St Loman's. No personal habit is left unnoticed. Hanna's trajectory through employment in Britain is driven as much by her desire for home as it is by an aversion to discomforts which seem to evoke unendurable memories. For instance, she leaves one post to move into London in search of 'love and adventure'. There she works, ironically in a monastery, where status, respect and a caring environment is afforded her. Six months later she is gone because, as she tells us, she could not bear the silent, miserable lives of the monks. Later again, she flees her hospital job following an encounter with a dead baby. We feel immense relief when she finds a home and security as a housekeeper with Dr Joseph. It is no surprise then that loss here too, when it comes, is catastrophic. Here, in her depiction of grief, we can see the power of her writing. She neither flinches nor escapes into self aggrandisement. Her voice is bold and confident, without shame or doubt.

Using that same skill, Hannah moves on swiftly to her last-recounted housekeeping post – in a fly-infested castle somewhere in Ireland. Her departure from this castle within a matter of days closes the book and, as it turns out, closes the written account of the life of Hanna Greally, keeper of stories and voice of many voiceless spirits of endurance.

Dr Eilís Ward, School of Political Science and Sociology,
National University of Ireland, Galway
September 2009

Part One

Coolamber Manor:
The Rehabilitation Story

Arrival at Coolamber

I spent about a year at Coolamber Manor, and my arrival there lives in my memory still. As I taxied up the long drive I noticed giant trees torn out of the earth, their roots beseeching the sky. Then I glimpsed a half haggard of hay, and to my savannah mind it appeared to have been there untouched for a very long time. I noticed long vacant stables, no horses to be seen, no thunder of hooves to be heard. One lone palm tree stood nearby. I dismissed the taxi and it crawled back down the gravelly drive to the white gates. I lifted my bags and started to ascend the steps slowly to the hall door of the Blue House.

Before I had climbed to the last step, the door was opened wide and a lady in reading glasses stood there welcoming me. This was the President. She was fairly tall, very erect and slim, with a nice smile. She wore country tweeds and I immediately wove her into the countryside of my imagination as a homely, tweedy pillar of normality. I smiled and gave my name. I learned that I was the fifth student to arrive and henceforth I became in all official documents, and for all numerical purposes, Number Five. The President, though, always addressed me as Johanna, and for some reason this pleased me. I stepped inside, leaving behind the soft fresh peaty air of October, the distant hills and the purple evening. The President showed me the dormitory I was to occupy. She excused herself graciously, leaving me to unpack. I looked around the dormitory appreciatively: soft pink candlewick spreads lay luxuriously on four single beds; gay chequered curtains, pleasantly geometric yet charmingly transparent, hung at the windows.

As I unpacked and filled my own wardrobe, shelves and locker I heard the voices of the rest of the students arriving. Their different accents sounded quaint and pleasant. They came from all parts of Ireland – Kerry, Mayo, Dublin; every corner. There were two girls from New Ross in County Wexford, one of them a Murphy. Irish dignity forbade the changing of Christian names and surnames to anything less conventional just now, but later on we were all to be given our nicknames by the Dublin Jackeen. She was the equivalent of *Burke's Peerage* in Coolamber. She named the Mayo Goats, the Kerry Bulldogs, the Yellow Bellies, the Galway Blazers, the Corkonians and so on. I was simply the Bulldozer.

I was introduced to my room mates and I liked them. Pain and suffering and miracles had brought us together. We said grace after our meal that evening in unison and gave thanks for God's mercy and love. We were the first pioneers of female rehabilitation in Ireland, and now we began to wonder about our fellow students. One girl seemed imperturbably happy and nobody guessed she was deaf until she used her hearing aid. Another was recovering from a tracheotomy with complications, but she was the gayest and most vivacious of us all. Her extreme youth, fifteen, and her very petulance endeared her to us because she had courage, did not mince her words in discussions and ignored all rules delightfully. I shall call her the Saint in this story because she was christened after a saint who also suffered greatly from asthma. But let incidents and circumstances introduce these girls as the story of Coolamber progresses.

That same evening in the recreation room the President gave out the Rosary to us. We knelt and murmured the prayers, and our eyes lifted occasionally to the erect blue-cloaked figure of the Madonna high up on a shelf. Our Lady represented our queen and mother, and somehow we all felt rested, peaceful and happy. The first day at Coolamber was nearly over; soon sleepy heads would rest on snow-white pillows and tongues would cease their chatter. Darkness would obliterate everything but our memories. The day's happenings slipped one by one from my sleepy mind. All that remained now was one thought – I had arrived.

Aims and Purposes

The President and her teachers were pioneers also in the praiseworthy task of training and sending out into the world girls who, were it not for misfortune, would be perfect. The students possessed to a noticeable degree courage and grit, in spite of great difficulties and handicaps. Each student was given special duties and responsibilities and I became official bellringer in the morning. The bell I rang was not much bigger than a Canterbury bell, but its compelling little tinkle was effective. It was my duty as long as I was at Coolamber to ring Rising Bell and also to call the staff from their slumbers. Breakfast was at eight o'clock and then we did our allotted share of the household tasks until about eleven o'clock, after which we went to a lecture; in those first days at Coolamber these were on handcrafts. The aims of these handcrafts, apart from their sale value, were, I believe, to develop manual dexterity, to encourage a constructive spirit and to develop independence. We all made friends with the teaching staff at these lectures and demonstrations. We also made friends with each other. Bonds of friendship were strengthened whenever one girl, perhaps with an awkward handicap, was helped and encouraged by another student to complete her rushwork. All the lectures and classes were well organised and in full swing before winter and the snows came. Hands and fingers became flexible and experienced, and the long electric fire in the craft room made lectures cosy and pleasant.

The rushwork was taught by one of the nicest people in

Longford. Her favourite saying, when somebody had achieved something difficult, was 'Good for you'. We all loved Mrs Good-for-you. Later on, when she started lecturing on poultry, her popularity increased even more because this was a subject everybody at Coolamber loved. One day at class she gave me a question on poultry and I musingly gave my opinion that different cocks should be used to avoid monotony. There was a roar of laughter at this from the students, but I had been quite serious.

As time went on we attended about five lectures a week in practical cookery and two or three in cookery theory. Practical cookery classes were recipes, method and demonstrations one day, followed the next day by the practical application of the lesson and by our cooking what had been demonstrated to us. Miss Honey was our youngest teacher, and she appreciated willingness and had a very good sense of humour. To read the Saint's notes required a sense of humour; to correct them required patience. With the Saint 'Great' was always 'Grate', but what intrigued me most was the word 'Brest' in her notes on poultry. 'Brest is a town in France', I said, but as I read on I realised she was alluding to the tender breast of chicken. Geography was not her strong point either, I discovered. Her most puzzling mistake or misapprehension was 'indication bird'. She was in a brown study one day, grimly concentrating on trying to make out her notes, and she called out to me, 'Joan, what is an indication bird?'

'Well, gosh,' I said, 'I never heard of it. Show me.' After much comparing of notes I realised her mistake. In my own notes the sentence ran: 'If the bird has a bright eye, it is an indication of tenderness.' I painstakingly explained the meaning of all this to the Saint. Her notes were always a revelation in terms of sheer inventiveness, but in time she was to become a good plain cook and a wonderful confectioner.

One of the nicest men in Coolamber was Sweet William, as we will call him to preserve his anonymity. He was that pillar of reliability and stoicism sometimes called the humble jack of all trades. He nursed Coolamber, as it were, in its cradle and before Coolamber opened he was caretaker and agricultural advisor and became the manager's indispensible right-hand man. After spending twenty years in hospital himself, he overcame his medical history and performed Herculean tasks to prepare Coolamber and to make it the lovely college it became. He loved both it and the students. His respectful unselfish devotion to the President was inspiring, and he consulted her in all matters, even technical ones.

Strictly speaking, there was no hierarchy at Coolamber, but, naturally enough, there was some competitiveness. The first students, or the 'pioneers', who had arrived in October were called Group A. The second group of girls, which arrived in January, was called Group B. The third group, which arrived in May and was the last I met because by then I had completed my time, was Group C. In the recreation room the three groups mixed indiscriminately, at least until a question of rank arose. Then factions became fiercely clannish and loyal. The different groups attended different lectures, elementary and advanced according to experience and how long they had spent at Coolamber. So for the moment I shall discuss Group A, the first pioneer group of girls who came to Coolamber in October, including yours truly.

Group A

As I breathed in the soft bog air of Coolamber, as I looked out from the library window, beyond the contented cattle grazing in the field to the distant smoke-blue hills, I contrasted the lovely copper beech outside with the one solitary palm tree that had always fascinated me. My mind flew to the Crusades. I thought, this is truly a country of ancient things, like this old palm tree, the first I had ever closely inspected and touched.

Coolamber was in County Longford and I became interested in the story I had read about its famous son, the Blessed Paul Mary Pakenham. He was the second son of the Earl of Longford and a soldier like St Ignatius Loyola and St Martin of Tours. He lived here in Longford, I thought to myself, the nephew of the Duke of Wellington and a convert to boot. He entered the Passionist Order and, although he had great learning and military success, he preferred lay duties to intellectual. I mused on about him. I was named after a soldier, too, St Joan. What strange sympathy or destiny had brought me to these soldier-hallowed places? Then there was the sword. One would not have expected to see a sword at Coolamber, but there was one. Long and rusty, it lay on the bottom shelf in the still room. Perhaps it had been used in the Crusades; perhaps Paul Mary Pakenham had used it himself; perhaps it was once red with the blood of infidels. I lifted it up, loved it, kissed it theatrically, and realised then that rehabilitation is a battle. This sympathy I felt was intensified later when the blue college uniform coats arrived. A picture of St Joan was on the tags, St Joan in armour with a long sword just like the one in Coolamber. Later on, when we were all invited to Pakenham Hall, Blessed Paul Mary's ancestral home, I saw similar swords hanging in the great hall. Shall flint ever be brought to such swords again? God only knows!

It was still October. We went by car to Mass on Sundays and on holidays, until we got our new bus with Coolamber College written on it in red. It was a nice creamy shade and P.T., our chauffeur, was young, gay and charming. The bus seated fourteen students and he held the door for us until we all climbed in. As the fourteenth sat down, he invariably said 'Twenty-eight legs, that's enough.' He must be quite a connoisseur of legs and nylons by now. Now Coolamber has two buses that make four or five runs to Mass, and also takes some girls to the Protestant service on a Sunday. P.T. fell in love about six times while I was there, 'many were called but few were chosen', and he still retains his bachelorhood lightheartedly. He drove us to church, to films, dances, on trips to the city, to shows and to the local village for our weekly shopping. I cycled short journeys myself, but in dubious weather or for anything over five miles I resorted to the college bus. It was very cosy and comfortable in the bus, especially when it was raining and the girls would sing the latest pop songs or old Irish melodies. When the President accompanied us she took the seat of honour at the front of the bus, accompanied by another teacher.

The President and Autumn

I could almost devote a whole chapter to the President, but I think she would prefer to be in the background of my account. But in Coolamber she could never be that. Her personality impressed me. She was, behind the scenes, a brilliant organiser and dispenser of justice. Her standards were high and the standards she set for the students were honest, unwavering and purposeful. Her talks and advice helped us and spurred us on to greater efforts. She had a swift, understanding smile, and when she smiled you felt happy; but if she had occasion to frown and disapprove, we had to apologise and try to improve. She was our President and all of us without exception liked and respected her greatly. Some students, rather young of

3/2173587

course, developed crushes on their teachers and loved them to such a degree that they could tell us what they were going to wear next! The quiet affection I, and all the students, had for the President, and she had for us, was heart-warming and sincere.

As with us, so with everybody else; she inspired a spontaneous respect and regard. When the Coolamber guild of the Irish Countrywomen's Association was formed, she was unanimously elected its presiden, too. That was the opinion of about fifty or sixty country women. They listened to her speeches and recognised her worth as a guild leader and organiser, and they greatly admired her brilliant interpretations of social welfare. She understood country women and she understood her students. Often, in the correction of some misdemeanour, she truly combined mercy with justice. A student was given three chances at least to reform and turn over a new leaf. She ordered life sweetly for us.

The October wind, in its haphazard fashion, swept up the fallen leaves, some 'pale crimson and hectic red', as the poet puts it, then left them to their own devices. Coolamber was beginning to take on a new aspect. All the remaining apples were taken from the apple trees in the old orchard and the last windfalls were stored on stone shelves in a house of their own. We students found new diversions every day. It was quite usual for students to visit the orchard for their walks and to come back to the house with pockets bulging with apples, which were generously handed around to the stay-at-homes. For my part, apples never tempted me, but I found pleasure in the pear tree. When jam-making was the order of the day we all went out to the old orchard and gathered the windfalls in boxes and baskets to make apple jelly and apple butter. Personally, I felt that the grapes were not appreciated enough: millions of lovely fresh black grapes, rather small but none the less delicious. Once or twice on a Sunday I broke off a nice glistening bunch and left them on the President's table as an additional course to her repast. She did not ask who was the donor, but I could see that she enjoyed them.

One autumn day the orchard suddenly disappeared. One day I was walking through a labyrinth of apple trees; the next there was the sound of bulldozers. These changed the orchard in a few days into a fertile brown field. There is a new orchard planted today in front of the house, not hidden at the back as the old one was. The trees, I was told, will bear fruit in about two years' time: cherry trees, plum trees, apple trees and others will soon greet visitors with a glow of colour and ripe fruit. But the old is still retained with the new. The old grapevine still gives abundant black grapes every harvest but today these are companioned by tomato plants and delicious peaches, while geranium pots give a splash of red. Thanks to the common labour of students and outdoor staff alike, there grows now in the old orchard rhubarb, potatoes, turnips, leeks, celery, fennel, lavender, parsley, herbs; in fact, all the country favourites.

The young disabled students at Coolamber had an unexpected courage, more so when they were very young and full of fun. This courage was in fact what I first noticed about all my fellow students – the will to do the job, even if clumsily in some cases, their laughter at frustrations and awkwardnesses. They were jolly, carefree, teasing. They were quick to sing, to dance and to make merry.

Slimming was the fashion at Coolamber. If you were not slim you could not wear slacks, and if you did not look well in slacks you could never hope to be the best dancer of the Twist. This was the overriding desire of nearly all of the teenagers there. The Saint was one of the best Twist-dancers in the place, at least until a girl known as Tension came. Tension belonged to Group C, a later group of arrivals, and she twisted until

23

everybody else dropped of exhaustion and admitted defeat. My own shortcomings in the Twist were overlooked and instead I was accepted as a fresh-air fiend.

A student of my Group A, whom I shall call Timmy, kept up regular slimming exercise although she had an artificial limb. She watched her diet, exercised regularly and kept a weather eye on the scales. I was in the kitchen one evening when Timmy rushed in, ignoring the handful of students in the kitchen, threw off her artificial limb, put the weights on the scales and weighed the prosthesis anxiously and carefully. Astonished at this peculiar behaviour, I said: 'Timmy, what's the matter?'

Still looking anxious, she took the hand off the scales, put it on herself and replied disgustedly, 'The big scales must be broken. I am two pounds heavier than last week and I worked so hard.' Then she added hopefully: 'Of course, I may have left my hand off last week.'

The last days of October were close. Jam and chutney were made now, and potted and stored, lectures went on and the rules of domestic science noted: everything cold for pastry, meals hot, how to serve the silver service and how to remove it, how to arrange a low attractive display of flowers, how to clean silver, the coffee pot was not to be mistaken for the water jug, a cheese knife was not a decorated lethal weapon and so on. The cheese knives at Coolamber were beautiful – curved, shiny silver blades with wonderful mother-of-pearl handles.

After Domestic Economy we welcomed the rush work class as a pleasant diversion. We made St Brigid's crosses out of fresh Shannon rush, as well as tablemats, baskets, breadbaskets and many other objects. All the tablemats used at Coolamber were made by the Group A students. There is a new crafts teacher in Coolamber now and she has introduced canework, weaving and rug-making with great success. She arrived in my last term. She is a very talented teacher and her canework cradles, baskets and trays are very beautiful.

Halloween

The leaves were tumbling down still, except from the Lombardy poplar trees. These towering trees, from which legend has it the True Cross was made, stood beside the Blue House like sentinels, or even more like witches' brooms. At Halloween a witch surely hovers over these brooms and scans the changing sky. She rides high and soars above them, disdaining the russet leafy carpets of Mother Earth.

The President decided to give a Halloween party for the students. Soon we were all making barm bracks, and apple cakes from the very best apples of the old orchard. Nuts, sweets and minerals were bought as extras for the party. Every student helped with the preparation, cooking and table service. Finally, the 'artists' were selected by Miss Honey, our Domestic Science teacher. These students hollowed out turnips and cut eyes, noses and mouths in them to transform them into life-like lanterns. Lighted candles were then stood inside them.

The party was a success and I must give credit for this to the genius of the President. No electric lights were switched on, and on tables, mantelpieces and shelves, mellow candle-light illuminated the laughing skulls of our scooped-out turnips. The effect gave a cosy but eerie feel to this ghostly season of Halloween. The next day would be All Souls' Day and winter would stalk abroad.

As the party came to a close some students started the refrain 'Roses are red, my love, violets are blue, ou – ou – ou', and we all joined in. This is the song that I associate with Coolamber more than any other. At parties, in our bus, at recreation, it was almost our signature tune. Our first party had been a happy, joyous one. The students had laughed, cracked nuts, crunched apples and danced. Ten or twelve hearty and attractive men had been invited, and young girlish eyes had laughed into male eyes, big feet and small feet had tapped and danced in unison. It had been a whirling, smiling world apart.

Winter came. Elvis Presley became the pin-up for the teenagers in Coolamber. We occasionally went to a film in the college bus. November lasted as winter months do, long, monotonous, no sunshine around the corner, nothing outside only deep mounds of sodden leaves, the lowing of the cattle in the sheds waiting to be milked by hand. Milking machines would not come until after Christmas. The November gales were guaranteed to loosen many slates, especially at the stables, whose days were numbered. The wind buffeted the trees. Coolamber Wood, across the fields, groaned and creaked. Mighty timbers towered dismally into the sky, and the fallen trees lying beneath made visitors scarce there. In November Coolamber Wood is different, almost menacing, and the wind-lashed trees are spectre-like and uninviting.

I often cycled to the little church two miles away to do the Stations of the Cross for the Holy Souls, and to pray before the Blessed Sacrament. I enjoy cycling, as mechanised vehicles – cars and the like – disagree with me. I always volunteered to cycle small journeys, weather permitting. As I cycled to the church to help the Holy Souls the wind whipped my cheeks to a rosy glow and, as always, I felt a sense of freedom and well-being out of doors. My lecture notes would come to my mind as I cycled along: 'Everything cold for rough puff pastry; caviar is always served with brown bread and a slice of lemon.' Or lectures on wood perhaps: 'Rolling pins are made from oak; also sieves.' Then again the pedals would change my thoughts to a poultry lecture: 'Rhode Island Red crossed with Leghorn – a good breed.'

Visitors to Coolamber

Members of the Irish Countrywomen's Association came some-times to visit Coolamber and they were always welcome. Students would receive visitors on Saturday or Sunday from 3 p.m. to 5 p.m. and might give them tea. Relatives came as well as strangers, tourists and patrons of Coolamber to see the place. As I was considered a good talker I was often appointed as guide on these tours.

One day we were all excited by the news that a lady and gentleman had come to televise Coolamber and its students. We stood at the mirrors with powder and puffs, our chattering only stopping long enough for us to apply our lipstick.

'Will lipstick show on television?'

'Mascara shows, I saw it.'

'What I can't understand is how girls can cry on television, and cry real tears.'

'Maybe someone will ask me to cry.'

'Good Heavens, my comb!'

Finally we all assembled in the various departments to be filmed. I was holding a bottle of green colouring for the first picture and I lifted a beautiful red casserole from the oven for another. In the rushwork room the girls were shown making St Brigid's crosses. Another day, two newspaper photographers came to photograph the students at work. I still have that picture, which I cut out of the paper.

One evening in November we were told that the ICA was forming a guild in the district and that it was at Coolamber that the meetings were to be held each month. They held their first big meeting there in the large recreation room. Our President became their president too and a better person could not have been chosen. The President's addresses and speeches were always indicative of considerable wisdom and executive ability in organisation and administration. She spoke frankly and naturally to us all and could sometimes tell a very good joke. The ICA meetings had their amusing side. Two or three students and myself joined the ICA and I still have the little badge, which I proudly display at meetings. Competitions were held at each meeting. Once, a prize was offered for the 'best-dressed wooden spoon'. I dressed my spoon in a new yellow duster with some green and tartan material around it to complete the ensemble. My spoon was much admired, but it did not win. Afterwards I spent hours trying to scrub it clean of lipstick, eye shadow and eyebrow pencil. Sometimes at the meeting the President showed a travel film; once a Bord na Mona film was screened. These meetings of the ICA were a pleasant diversion for us all.

Sometimes we were visited by rehabilitation officers. They were handsome, kind men doing a good job and bringing happiness to hundreds. They talked to us and laughed and joked and always had a word of praise or encouragement. Our favourite was Uncle K. He did not know it but he was called Uncle K by an admiring group of students at Coolamber. (The K is because I do not know if he likes publicity.) He knew each student personally and followed their progress carefully. He knew their defects and limitations, but he also knew their capabilities. He interviewed students regularly and advised them on their choice of training and employment. We students instinctively knew that Uncle K had a deep sympathy for us, and we reciprocated this feeling by unofficially adopting him into our circle of friends.

Our Progress

Our teachers monitored our progress all the time, carefully and unobtrusively assessing a talent here, noting a special aptitude there, spotting a young flagging heart perhaps in need of encouragement and help. We all received this help and encouragement at Coolamber, from the President especially. The President and the teachers seemed to have been selected for their special skills and abilities, and they inspired love and affection in their charges. The students themselves were fine young people, and if sometimes they were cross, irritable or snappy, you easily forgave them, for at heart they were brave and cheerful, though awkward, handicapped and mentally or physically hurt at times.

Someone else who should be mentioned for conveying to us at all times a subtle encouragement was that most charming and lovable person, Mrs Good-for-you. Smiles would break out when she began, 'Good. . .' – And 'For you!' we would finish in chorus. She never minded our exuberance; in fact she encouraged it. She was a tonic to us, and she knew the value of cheerful spirits. She was also very forbearing with slow-to-learn students. The most important thing about Mrs Good-for-you was that she loved us, and we loved her. It was as simple as that.

The teachers really knew their students. One might wonder why one girl was with the calves indefinitely, but nobody questioned the President's wisdom. She knew what was good for each student and she acted accordingly. I was often placed in charge of the laundry because I was reliable as regards the machinery there. Also I was often praised for the linen I laundered.

We girls were thinking about our futures. Some of us liked poultry, some confectionery and some office work. The general tendency in the first and second terms was to study everything, discount nothing and reserve judgement. We were a happy-go-lucky, carefree lot, interdependent and content with each other's company. We all looked forward to the one film, the one dance, the same television show. Still we found time to write up our notes and study a little each night. There was some desperate cramming though, among the intelligentsia, for the mid-term tests. Hot black coffee and head swathed in wet towels is what I advocate for these last-minute crammers. However, mid-term tests were one thing, but most of us were aghast at the mere mention of the final Diploma. I came third in my first term but then wound up first in my last term. I got highest marks in Cookery and Theory, and honours in all subjects. I was also 'specially mentioned' and highly commended for maintaining a good average.

Preparations for Christmas

Time rolled on. November dripped on into December and we learned that Coolamber was to be vacated, except for Sweet William, for a week at Christmas. The poultry were not coming until January and so it was thought that the expense of a staffed house was unnecessary, especially as most students had homes to go to. One was going west, another east, another south. 'Home Sweet Home', naturally, became the most popular tune.

It was announced that a Christmas dinner was to be held before we went on holidays.

From now on all our thoughts and actions revolved around the coming of Christmas. Every second day we made Christmas cakes and plum puddings, and classes became a mixture of industry and anticipation. The pungent smell of brandy and whiskey filled the kitchen. There was also the nostalgic smell of a Christmas cake baking in the oven for five hours. One smelt the sharp scent of apples, as an apple was always put into each cake to make it dark and moist. We learned the professional way to clean fruit, the way to enhance aromatic flavours by correct mixing. Egg-beaters whirred, creaming machines revolved; nuts were blanched while dates, fruit and lemon peel were all chopped and saturated with aromatic glasses of whiskey or brandy, or sometimes wine. Our spirits soared, too, among the homely kitchen smells and Christmas preparations, and hope was born anew in our breasts. We thought of home fires, turkey, plum pudding and the shrill cries of children exclaiming, 'Look what Santa brought me!'

We worked with a will and when the cakes were ready for icing we topped each, in our imaginations at least, with our chosen figures: the bride and groom, Santa, reindeer, sledges and the Bethlehem star. The mind was an inexhaustible source of creation for us. We cut stars and shapes from green angelica, coloured almonds with cochineal and green colouring. We were, in fact, studying and practising our first lessons in specialised confectionery. Miss Honey was a wonderful confectioner herself – her cakes were magnificent to behold – and classes progressed happily under her expert guidance and instruction.

I was to be the sole student who had no home to go to. My parents were long dead and the last I heard of my home was that it had been burnt to the ground. My family were scattered and I was in a dilemma.

Two weeks before Christmas Uncle K came to Coolamber on his usual fortnightly business to inspect the farm, financial reports and other matters. I knew he would help me if I told him I had nowhere to go for the holidays. First of all I asked the President if I could have a personal interview with Uncle K. This was arranged. I went into the library to find Uncle K there in front of a lovely log fire. He asked me to sit down and rather nervously I began.

'I have nowhere to go for the holidays, Mr K, and Coolamber is closing.'

Kindly and encouragingly he asked me where I would like to go and had I anything in mind. I told him that I would like to stay the week in Dublin at a hotel, rest, go to pantomimes, museums, art galleries – and to the zoo, too, I added laughing. He said he would see what he could do and would speak to the President about me. He was satisfied, if it could be arranged, that I would be happy doing these things, and the interview came to a happy conclusion.

A few days later the President told me that Rehabilitation would book me in for a week at a good hotel. I was so delighted I could hardly wait to tell the news. I was very happy in Coolamber, of course, but even so I was infected by the general excitement and delightedly joined in the helter-skelter of selecting one's best clothes for packing. There was the planning, the saving out of an allowance. Train times were looked up and the well-thumbed Transport Book was passed around as early as two weeks before we went away.

Christmas

The early Christmas dinner at Coolamber on 18 December was to be the biggest social event for us so far. I started up a collection for gifts to put under the Christmas tree and I met with a generous response from all. The tree was hewn from Coolamber land. I will always remember our Christmas dinner because it was truly a lively occasion, attended by all the grace and elegance of kindly courtesy. I am certain the other students of my Group A will never forget the unselfish devotion and affection of the President and her teachers; neither will they forget, I am sure, the warmth and friendship of Coolamber, especially at that Christmastide.

Plans began to be set in place for the elaborate dinner. It did not knock a feather off Miss Honey, who was quite used to such things. She showed us the menu and told us the general programme plans. The menu was as follows, printed in tiny gold letters:

> Hors d'oeuvres
> Consommé à la Julienne
> Turkey, Ham, Brussel sprouts, Potatoes, Stuffing,
> Bread sauce, Brown sauce, Cranberry sauce
> Plum pudding and Brandy butter
> Sherry trifle
> Coffee

There were to be liqueurs served in the lounge for the staff and visitors and expensive minerals for the students. A little wine was allowed to students who were over twenty-one, as well as a sherry aperitif.

A monstrous turkey was produced in the kitchen by Miss Honey, who then demonstrated to us how to draw the sinews. Incisions were made in the gaiter-covered leg of the turkey cock and deftly he was delaced, as we saw it. After the bird was ready for the oven we were all assigned jobs. I was given the fascinating job of preparing the ham, which was almost as monstrous as the turkey. As I skinned it and stuck in the cloves in the traditional pattern, I thought how much it resembled chainmail.

Invitations were sent out. Ten extra guests were expected. I was given the consommé à la Julienne to prepare, then I made bread sauce and cranberry sauce. After that I was ordered to go upstairs and change into something suitable, as I was to be the wine waiter. I took off my cookery apron and gave a sigh of relief. This was a job I would enjoy, I thought: going round the tables with a bottle of wine or liqueurs and a napkin, pouring the bright liquids into beautiful crystal glasses. I visualised myself as a sort of head waiter, perhaps at the Savoy, discreet and respectful. Thus I was initiated into the secrets, or rather the fundamentals, of wine courses. There was hock, Sauterne, cherry brandy and many others. I disdained to taste them, but I sniffed them once or twice to show that I knew the power of a wine's bouquet, although nobody paid much attention to me.

The many tables were laid, all joined together in a large horseshoe shape under two huge cloths. The table linen and silver were immaculate. The students were all dressed up under their blue nylon coats ready for the dance afterwards. The coats were perfect; I had laundered them myself for the occasion. The Saint was the receptionist for the evening. At last the visitors arrived, a little before seven, laden with parcels for the Christmas tree. The Saint showed them into the lounge, where I and some other students helped them hang their presents on the tree. The tree was brilliantly lit with little coloured bulbs, and sparkled with tinsel and imitation snow. Refreshments and aperitifs were served in the lounge. On the low lacquered tables were tiny dishes with delicacies of sweet-meats and olives on sticks. The Saint's boyfriend was dressed up as Santa Claus, and he was not long there until we guessed his identity. After much hand-shaking, well-wishing and exclaiming over the lovely tree, dinner was announced.

Just at that moment the electric lights were extinguished by order of the President, and Coolamber took on a new ambiance. Instead of electricity, there was candlelight. Christmas candles, red, blue and white, glowed softly on tiny frost-decorated yule logs placed casually but effectively on windows and mantelpieces, in the hall and on the Christmas table. They dominated the scene, those candles, and we discovered that candlelight is flattering to all ages. We said grace and started dinner. First I had to serve the hock and then I sat down to my soup where a card indicated my place. Everything was well organised and dinner proceeded smoothly, wines were sipped, minerals fizzed and youthful thirsts were slaked. Thoughts and feelings mellowed. A speech was made by the President while I, unexpectedly, was selected by the unanimous acclamation of the students to speak on their behalf. My speech was impromptu but I received a good ovation. The President charmed everyone with her usual *savoir-faire* and command of language and expression. Her speech, unusually youthful, contributed immensely to our enjoyment of the dinner. 'Not on bread alone doth man live.'

When the speeches were over, a toast was drunk to the President and Coolamber. Then, after much clapping, the President and her guests retired to the lounge. Meanwhile, the students and all the available males helped clear the tables and prepare the hall for the dance. There was plenty of music; we had two or three accordionists and a new record player. Some danced non-stop until one o'clock on that starry, frosty morning. The President and the guests came into the dance later on and joined with the 'Paul Jones' and the old-time waltzes. There was also much Twisting to please the teenagers. The last item on the programme was, of course, 'Auld Lang Syne', when everybody joined hands and sang the old refrain, 'Let auld acquaintance be forgot for the sake of auld lang syne'. It felt like Christmas already, and indeed it was our own special Christmas, even though it was still a week to Christmas Day. We felt very happy during it all and the thought of the week's holiday in three days' time made us absolutely delirious.

The results of the Christmas tests in Theory and Practical were pinned up for all to see on the green notice board the next day. Two other students had come first and second by a mark or two, but I saw with relief that I was a close third. After all, I was much older than the others. And then, at last, the day of the holidays arrived. I went by train as far as Dublin with our President. From there she was going south and we said our goodbyes at my hotel. She wished me a happy Christmas as she left.

I enjoyed my week in Dublin. I went to Mass and Communion every morning. I breakfasted in the American style for fun, having coffee instead of tea. I used the 'double pour' that I had been taught, though I was surprised to notice that the coffee drinkers around me did not. Even an American poured coffee first and then added the cream. I visited museums and art galleries in the morning and I went to pantomimes in the evening after the Rosary. I will always remember the pantomime *Goody Two Shoes* with amusement. I had received a box of chocolates in the post and, as I clapped in the dark, my chocolates tipped over and I lost half the boxful.

On Christmas Eve I visited the living crib at St Martin's and then lit a candle in my room. On Christmas Day I attended three Masses. A very funny fat man danced, or tried to dance, the Twist at the hotel. Later on in the day I went to two parties, and wore a paper hat and pulled crackers, and ate plenty of turkey, plum pudding and trifle. After Christmas I visited the zoo, Dublin Castle and Christ Church, where the organ was being played. All during Christmastide Dublin was lit up like a fairyland.

The trip to Dublin passed all too quickly for me and then I had a note from Uncle K offering to give me a lift back to Coolamber, as he was going down on business. I was very pleased by this friendly gesture, quite apart from the fact that it saved me the pound train fare.

A New Term

It was January now and I mentally took stock again of Coolamber, for this was to be my second term. I was the first to arrive but within a couple of days all the others had come back too. This was the month when thousands of day-old chicks were expected and also, of course, a new group of students.

We congregated again in the dear old lounge and conversation began. Some of the students had learned to dance the 'Locomotion' in the holidays, others had not quite mastered it and gave their own weird interpretations. Some students had had love affairs. They passed around glamorous photos of the latest boyfriend and spoke pityingly of their former selections. Everybody had some news to tell and afterwards we all settled down again to another term of domestic science.

Snow fell a few days later, the day the new students were expected in the afternoon. I was selected to show them to their dormitory, to help carry their bags and help them unpack. Two of the new girls were to occupy two vacant beds in my dormitory. T was from New Ross and Rose was from Kilkenny. They were the sweetest girls and we became very fond of each other. T wanted to be a nun and Rose was up for anything. Now I had almost a saint and almost a desperado for my sleeping partners! The rest of the new group were again from all over Ireland – Cork, Laois, Kildare. One girl came from Tipperary 'far away" and she got so homesick that she refused to stay. We all gathered around her in consternation at her obvious distress. We tried to cheer her up, we told her she was tired and would feel better tomorrow, but she was adamant. Between sniffs, she informed us that she would return immediately to Tipperary. The President had a cup of tea with her and spoke consolingly, but to no avail. Her only concession was that she would go home the next morning instead of there and then.

Apart from the girl from Tipperary, there was no self-pity about this Group B that I was aware of. They had 'screwed their courage to the sticking point', as Shakespeare says. Three had crutches, two had splints. The girls on crutches amazed me with their happy expressions and cheerful philosophy: 'We must creep before we walk' and so forth. One girl had irons on both legs, as she was recovering from polio. Her acrobatic antics and Twisting were actually talented. She was also to become excellent with her hands and produce lovely craft-work. She won prizes later on for her cradles, trays and baskets at the country shows.

As time went on I noticed the physical and mental improvement in the girls. Some were heroically overcoming handicaps, sometimes even forgetting them in the general mêlée of recreation. A number of students developed a talent for mimicry, which seemed to lighten their burdens.

As the last prayers of the Rosary were spoken by the President each evening one could almost hear, in the short silence afterwards, the hope beating in our hearts. Miracles did happen; that is to say, unofficial miracles, like renewed hope of complete recovery. There was one girl whom I shall call Zita. She had partial paralysis resulting from a domestic accident. She would sometimes confide in me. 'Joan,' she would say eagerly, massaging one of her hands, 'Joan, I must keep up the exercises. I actually feel the power and life coming back into it.' I would express delight and joy, and the sensitive young face with the high cheekbones would flush gently. I believe myself that hers was a slow-moving miracle of recovery. There had been a time in her life that was bitter indeed, when she had suffered from complete paralysis. Then gradually, as month succeeded month, power crept back into her frozen muscles and Zita came back to life, but slowly, so slowly. I longed and prayed for her complete recovery. Another time she would say, 'Joan, I know, I just know that some day I will be a hundred per cent.' One holiday she went to Lourdes and contracted ptomaine poisoning, of all things. But she came back even more lovable, and more faithful and persevering than ever. While at Lourdes she prayed for me and she wrote and told me so. She enclosed the following prayer, which I keep in my prayer book. It is my most cherished souvenir of her friendship.

'To Our Lady of Lourdes'

O Holy Virgin, in the midst of your days of glory, do not forget the sorrows of this earth. Cast a merciful glance upon those who are suffering, struggling against difficulties with their lips constantly pressed against life's bitter cup.

At this sentence I imagined Zita with 'life's bitter cup' pressed against her sensitive lips. The prayer continues:

Have pity on those who love each other and are separated.

Have pity on our rebellious hearts.

Have pity on our weak faith.

Have pity on those we love.

Have pity on those who weep, on those who pray, on those who fear.

Grant hope and peace to all. Amen.

I pray I will see her cured some day.

A Thousand Chickens Arrive

One day, to the delight of Mrs Good-for-you, the thousand chickens arrived. We all went out with her to see them and to take notes. Some students took up the fluffy little chicks and petted them. They looked so nice and so helpless, chirping feebly under the lovely warm brooder. Those girls who had an aptitude for poultry were assigned to poultry duties, filling automatic drinkers with water and feeders with meal. When the 'feathering day' was over their duty was to switch on the blue night light. The whirring ventilation fans revolved incessantly in the poultry shed. Coolamber's first commercial poultry farm was now in working order and its poultry students were having their first lessons in the care and management of fowl.

Poultry study was compulsory for everyone. We sometimes had quiz sessions and questions on poultry would be asked, such as: 'What does a hen do for teeth?' The answer, 'Grit her teeth', became a standing joke. At poultry lectures we learned the mysteries of the hen and her eggs from Mrs Good-for-you. We learned about the embryo, the interior strings of balance, moulting. We also learned medical remedies for the hens. We were shown how to clean, preserve and store eggs. We used the preserved eggs months afterwards for the confectionery unit.

Speaking of eggs, the hens began to lay six months later. Their first eggs were small, as is usual with pullets, but like everything else at Coolamber there was something special about our eggs, as the following little episode will show. One afternoon at a practical cookery class I went to the basket to use some eggs. I discovered one to be twins – two eggs in one shell. Our teacher was in very good humour over it and sent me down to show it, one of the very first eggs to be laid at Coolamber, to Mrs Good-for-you. I excitedly showed her the twins and she and I agreed that it was a prosperous omen for Coolamber, as indeed it turned out to be, for those twins were only the beginning. About one egg in every five had double yolks. The eggs were very plentiful and our cakes were all the richer for them. It was a long time before the eggs became single-yolked. Miracles happen at Coolamber sometimes and I am still hoping to see a triplet egg. So when Mrs Good-for-you reads this book, and please God she will, I hope she will send me an update.

Spring at Coolamber

Spring came in energetically. In February the Coolamber land became another source of discovery. My eyes strayed to the woods expectantly. I knew I would find there snowdrops and primroses, and I did. The snowdrops were not confined to the woods – they were in all sorts of odd places, in the fields and behind the old stables, too. They were unbelievably abundant and beautifully large and white. The days became a little longer and sometimes the sun would shine in the afternoons. When the lecture was over, and the four o'clock cup of tea, I often walked over to the woods and I was never disappointed. There were lovely yellow primroses, a plentiful supply always for gatherers. I could not believe that one wood could contain so many; the supply seemed inexhaustible. In a little wood at home, I remembered as a child a small vision of primroses, as if God had quietly opened a jewel case to me there beside the stream. I retained the memory of them intact for years, until now, because when dreams materialise, memories fade. Now I thought, God, what wealth you are showing me; this is not your old jewel case but an amazing treasure. The primroses grew and multiplied until May. As I sped along on my bicycle to the church, I often stopped and gathered a bunch to leave in the vase outside the rails at St Anthony's statue in Boherquill chapel.

The sap mounted higher and higher in the trees of Coolamber until they were restored to their pristine elegance. Buds appeared and the sweet bark held many secrets. The new orchard was planted now: plums, cherries, apples and pears. I was walking one evening in the garden and I entered the gate to where the old orchard had once flourished. There was not a sign of it now. The land was ploughed and Ginger, our horticultural and agricultural instructor, was there, trying to tie labels onto fruit trees. It was a most difficult task, I noticed, as he had the use of only one hand, the other being paralysed. I offered to help and the familiar ear-to-ear grin flashed as he thanked me. He showed me which trees to tie the labels to and told me that in two months' time they would be transplanted to newly ploughed land beside the front avenue. He told me that they would bear fruit in about two years' time. Ginger did a magnificent job at Coolamber, together with Sweet William and the other outdoor staff. With the use of

42

only one hand he ploughed the ninety-nine acres. He is truly outstanding in courage, a veritable hero. He recently married a sweet girl from the West and they have one beautiful baby boy so far.

Well, spring breezed on and very soon it was St Patrick's Day. This was another day of celebration for Coolamber. We had a party and a dance afterwards. A feast was laid out on tables covered with snow-white linen – apples, cakes, fruit-cakes, cream-and-jam cakes, sweets and desserts. Also on the table was my statue of St Patrick. On state occasions, as this was, I brought it down from the dormitory to add to the scene. I made snakes by colouring bananas and St Patrick banished them with a wave of his crosier.

I brought St Patrick down again the day we had the Stations at Coolamber and he was there on the day we celebrated Mass when the college was consecrated to the Sacred Heart by our very good pastor. We all received Holy Communion that day and enjoyed a communal breakfast afterwards with the staff and priest.

Lent came in, almost unnoticed, and soon, in our best sackcloth and ashes, we attended the Stations of the Cross every Tuesday and Friday in Boherquill church. We learned that there were to be Easter holidays for five days and that afterwards a new group of students would join us.

Mid-term Tests

Meanwhile our studies were getting more advanced. In Poultry we studied the crossing of breeds, egg structure and so on. In Domestic Economy we learned how to make home-made silver cleaner and polish, in which jeweller's rouge and white precipitate is used. I remember this because it sounded romantic to me. In Cookery we were now making cabinet pudding and choux pastry, which I adored. Cream buns, a favourite of mine, are made from that unaccountably lovely stuff.

The day of the Easter tests drew nearer. In the recreation room questions were constantly being asked and answered.

'Would a Group A student please advise a Group B student as to the preparation of chutney?'

Groans from Group A.

'Give us a rest. I did thirty pounds of chutney last term.'

Voice of genius from deep armchair: 'In red tomato chutney you shrivel the tomato, for green you halve it.'

Faint reply: 'Oh, I see.'

'Rose, a half teaspoon is not a pinch . . .'

Then the Dublin Jackeen screeches, 'Girls, it's Elvis!' and there is a mad rush to the TV. Eyes are glued on Elvis to the strains of 'Take these Chains from My Heart and Set Me Free'. Recreation begins and all academic queries and doubts are dismissed without a qualm. Elvis is more popular than Solomon in Coolamber.

The day dawned for the Practical Cookery test (and thus the Dublin Jackeen's hopes for some kind of divine intervention were dashed). Two girls were examined at a time. They went into the kitchen together and drew their questions from a number of slips prepared by Miss Honey. In my senior paper I was asked to cook a dinner for six. I made soup, roast lamb, peas, roast potatoes, redcurrant jelly, mint sauce and brown gravy sauce. We were there under the professional eye of Miss Honey. I wrapped greaseproof paper carefully around the leg of mutton, to prevent burning, as I hastened to make the sauces. Next, I diced my vegetables for the soup, as I had often noticed in class that it takes three times the time to purée vegetables as to dice them. Next, I made Bakewell tart and French cream cake. I finished and, relieved, noticed that there were still fifteen minutes left until the time was up. I served my food on silver dishes with doilies, happy that all had gone well. For that Easter test I received 71½ per cent.

Tea became a riot of laughter and good humour that afternoon. Now the tests were over we could relax. Through sips of tea we held the usual post mortem. Rose's case was discussed first. We knew Group B would have to prepare something elementary, but – my dear Watson! – her assignment had been to make scrambled egg. I asked her how she had made it and with much gesticulation she described her method. Everything seemed OK until she said 'And then I added the flavouring.'

'Flavouring? What kind of flavouring? Pepper and salt?'

'No,' she replied weakly, 'vanilla essence.'

The students nearby, who overheard this, roared with laughter. The story went around but it was supper time before her pal Mary heard it. I told her then of Rose's test. Mary had been tested in scrambled egg herself and was now eating it reheated. 'So that's it!' she exclaimed. 'This is the queerest scrambled egg I have ever had – it must be Rose's vanilla essence!' By supper time their scrambled eggs must have got mixed up in the heater.

Students had to answer twenty-two questions out of the twenty-four set for the Theory paper. There were questions on cookery, diet, menus, poultry, crafts, hygiene. I liked the paper and I got 70 per cent for it. I was 'specially mentioned' later for maintaining a good average in both Theory and Practical Cookery.

Tea came and was one of the funniest half hours I have ever spent. One or two *faux pas* were particularly amusing. Beatrice had been asked what was a bouquet garni and to our delight she told us she had written down the following: 'A bouquet garni is a great big fish in the Mediterranean.' I guessed that she had mixed it up with caviar. In the lecture on savouries Miss Honey had explained that caviar is from the roe of the sturgeon – but my analysis fails after that because I think caviar is exclusive to the Caspian Sea. The girls thought it was screamingly funny and screeches of laughter at Beatrice continued for quite ten minutes until T claimed our interest with her answer to the question 'What are man-made fabrics?' She had listed: 'Trousers, men's coats, men's this, that and the other.' More screams broke out and I hurriedly closed the communicating door to contain the noise.

Generally speaking, the questions on calories, diet and recipes were answered accurately. Everyone passed, some got honours and some a 'special mention'. We were also tested in rushwork, and, to my surprise, I got over 50 per cent and produced a very respectable table lamp in river rush.

Easter Holidays

We were relieved when the tests were all over and the talk was now of the approaching Easter holidays. One group was to go on holidays and the other group was to follow on their return.

I was corresponding at this time with a country cousin. She was a National School teacher, a principal, and she had visited me in February. She wrote and invited me to stay with her for five days at Easter. I was thrilled. This time I was going on holidays properly, to a relative whom I especially liked. She was quite a genius. It was not because she had been offered a position as clerical officer and been called to teaching simultaneously, but because she had actually got 100 per cent in mathematics, and to my mind that really is genius, in a girl especially.

Holy Thursday arrived and my cousin motored up to collect me. Again I said goodbye to Coolamber, and that evening found myself at evening Mass in the village church of my childhood. I had passed many a holiday in this country place. After Mass was over, while my cousin played the organ I surprised my grand-uncle by taking his arm, and we walked together like that to my cousin's house. I told him all my news and how I was staying with Cousin C for Easter. He was delighted in his kindly gruff way. I presented him with a green-rush St Brigid's Cross and told him that I had also sent one to another cousin, his youngest daughter, who was in Australia, so very far away this Holy Easter. I could see in my imagination the soft green-rush cross bringing happiness and tender memories of green Ireland to my cousin there.

The few days' holidays from Coolamber passed quickly. I revisited old places. One day, taking a short walk before lunch, I saw three dead animals in a ditch. I arrived back with the news that I had seen 'three beavers out yonder, in a ditch near a dam.' I was corrected by the locals, who said that some-body really ought to remove those 'perishing badgers'. I put up a stiff argument for the three being beavers, mentioning the water and signs of a dam, but eventually I yielded to the coun-trymen's opinion, and my vision of a beaver coat waiting out there for the skinning faded.

Easter Sunday was the nicest day of all, and then I pre-pared to return to Coolamber on the Tuesday of Easter Week. I motored back with Cousin C and I remember feeling lonely, but I braced myself for the new and final term. I was down on the Rehabilitation lists for employment in September.

There was much excitement when I returned. More girls were to arrive in three days' time, I learned. 'Group C!' we all chanted delightedly, and Groups A and B climbed up a few more rungs of the academic ladder and gazed down pityingly on the rookies in Group C. Students were seriously considering their futures now. Minds were made up, decisions were taken. Some girls liked dairy, some preferred poultry; cooks, confectioners, typists, all were choosing their prospective jobs. Coolamber was changing and so were we, developing from raw immaturity to confident maturity, from timid first-term students to trained young women determined to make a go of it in spite of handicaps. The last soft days of April passed, soaked with April showers.

Group C and the Notice Board

It was as fair as the flowers in May when Group C arrived, and with their arrival a new era began. Group A lectures were fewer but more advanced and more interesting. Practical application of theory was now our problem and we were asked to monitor, and sometimes supervise, the new girls. Group C occupied a wing of their own on the second floor. One dormitory was a lovely blue and the other a deep yellow. I had the duty, as usual, of seeing them to their respective dormitories and of helping them to carry up their baggage. I also had the duty of introducing them to the other students. I told them the rules briefly. The President herself talked to them later about rules and regulations. I showed them the notice board, the cause of many a laugh and prank. I pointed out the various notices: ICA meetings, amusement lists, bath lists, special assignments to students, forthcoming shows and results of tests.

The girls' duties for the week were sometimes put up on

the notice board late at night. One night I felt bored and mischievous. I looked into the neighbouring dormitories and called out, 'Girls, the list is up.' Then I addressed myself to a student who preferred cooking duties and I said, 'Pet, you're in the laundry.' This untruth was greeted by a groan of horror from Pet. God forgive me for my lie. Now students were beginning to take notice and look anxious, and exclamations like 'Heavens, where am I?' were heard. I retreated quietly as bedclothes were pushed back, dressing gowns and slippers hastily put on and there was a stampede down the stairs to the notice board. Of course, I knew that it was only the old list that was up and not the new one. I followed them down out of curiosity and to confess. I felt a little sorry for them, but it was too late. The perpetrators of pranks must not sympathise with their victims. So I grinned and remarked how nice everybody looked in their night attire.

To leave well enough alone is a good plan, but only a week later the Saint tried the same trick. As she was only sixteen, and unthreatening, the girls had no mercy. They went downstairs all right, but came back up furious and looking for the Saint. She tried hiding in the bathroom, which she could not lock, as she explained to me later. They easily pushed the door in and grabbed her and carried her back to her bed. There they unceremoniously removed her apparel and bounced her. She protested and roared vigorously and would have fought like a tiger, as was her custom, only she was hopelessly outnumbered.

'The President is coming!' I hissed.

The assassins all jumped into bed and so did the Saint, threatening revenge. Then she got out of bed again, put on her night attire, strode out and came back immediately with a glass of water in her hand, which she dashed into the faces of her assailants. The wars were really on after that for a fortnight, and nobody could remember how or why it had all started. But I did.

The Merry Month of May

May came in dressed in blue, a queenly blue like Our Lady's mantle, and we loved and acknowledged it. We put away our winter woollies and donned silk, satin, cotton, muslin and linen all in its honour. Our own dresses and blouses were covered by our uniform, our nylon coats the same colour as the blue sky of May. I was requested by the President to make a May altar on our floor. I was delighted with the privilege. When I had completed my handiwork, it was truly a charming little altar. We religiously tended it all through the month of May. There were still spring daffodils, and I gathered these for the first week or so of May until one day, as I stood with the scissors in my hand in the midst of a huge crowd of flowers, I saw that their pristine souls had fled. They no longer had the first dewy freshness of spring, and sadly I acknowledged that they were withered. I gathered very pale pink rhododendrons instead for the larger vases, and purple and yellow pansies for the tiny ones.

Coolamber was never without flowers. Prize roses preened against grey walls, exuding perfume and luxury. The wild Irish rose grew and grew on the garden walls, until one thought that the walls would fall down. There was one beautiful rose just outside the dining-room window, and on it a lovely yellow tea rose. Sometimes, I sat in the dining-room at a table facing it and, as I sipped my tea, I revelled in the beauty of this tea rose, so appropriately named for it seemed to add a subtle flavour and sweetness to my tea. Before the roses had come out at all, I had been watching for one to put on the President's table. At last I found a lovely dark crimson peony rose on a wall in the vegetable garden. I cut it and put it on her table in water and, to my delight, she said, 'Isn't it lovely?'

Uncle K came specially to Coolamber one day in May to interview the students individually. The President and Miss Honey were also there in the library. He asked us what we would like to do and what employment we would prefer. In certain cases a student's mind was divided between a choice of two occupations, as indeed was mine. Uncle K, the President and Miss Honey were most kind and helped me with the decision. As Coolamber was mainly a domestic science training college, one had a choice of the following occupations: cook, confectioner, housekeeper, waitress, poultry girl or dairymaid. I decided on the occupation of housekeeper. I was then written down for immediate employment in the autumn.

The die was cast. I thought of the girls who were remaining on for another year to specialise in confectionery, and thought that confectionery was certainly romantic and artistic. I thought of piling pristine icing onto beautiful cakes, making dozens of cream buns, but then I stopped and considered that my case was different. I was one of the oldest students at Coolamber. Teenagers might not mind staying on for another year, but I had waited years and years already for liberty, praying in hospital for it, and now Rehabilitation would give it to me. They would secure employment for me and I would be free again. I had had freedom in small cramped degrees but now I wanted it prodigiously and for ever. Again and again I thought of liberty. I longed to walk along by the sea, to feel the wind in my face and hair, to have to decide things for myself and to act in the living present. So I dreamed on; I would soon be a citizen, I would vote, earn money and perhaps become well off. God is very good.

It was my last term at Coolamber, I reflected sadly, but the buoyant, hopeful thought that I was going to be free again helped, and I thought, too, that perhaps I might even make a success of my life yet. What I really felt, though, was that I would place my trust in God. I was not sufficient unto myself. I prayed, and God consoled me with many happy reflections. One was that I was very fortunate that Rehabilitation had befriended me. I decided I would take orders for a time at least, but, I thought consolingly, at least my soul would be unfettered even though my body would be in service. Look at the saints, I thought, they had to conquer self. I was fortified by prayer and sayings such as: 'God helps those who help themselves'.

Pakenham Hall

Could it have been the hand of God that brought me to Coolamber, I once wondered. I had read the Blessed Paul Mary Pakenham's life some years before I arrived, while I was still in hospital. I had made a novena to him then for my usual request, liberty. He must have heard me, I thought, and perhaps my own saint, St Joan, and St Ignatius and Paul Mary are all friends above. Well anyhow, I thought he sounded very nice; and I was glad to be living in his home county of Longford.

Imagine my delight to hear one day that there was to be a garden fête at Lord Longford's house, Pakenham Hall, and the proceeds were to go to charity. Coolamber students were invited and were offered a stall there for raffles and also to sell craftwork. Three girls were to be in charge of the stalls while the remainder of us were to enjoy ourselves.

The garden fête was held on a lovely day in June. The sky was a cloudless blue and Pakenham Hall rested like a medieval castle on a soft green carpet of grass. I had expected to see an elaborate mansion; instead there was this fairy castle. The principal attraction of the day was a conducted tour of the castle. I eagerly decided to go on this and expected every minute that a miracle would happen.

First we came to the entrance, an ancient iron-studded door. While we waited for the guide to open it, I imagined Paul Mary as a small boy standing where we all stood now, pressing those heavy studs with his tiny fingers; I imagined him next as a soldier lifting the huge iron ornamental knocker. The door opened and we trooped inside the large hall. My eyes went first to a collection of toys and a faded spotted rocking horse. Then I saw a collection of swords hanging together in one corner. There were dozens of them – long ceremonial swords, curved swords, scimitars, some unsheathed and others in their scabbards. Both St Paul Mary and St Ignatius Loyola had started off with these weapons, but then St Ignatius had chosen a staff instead of a sword and Paul Mary had chosen a broom and a dishcloth! Both men met opposition, but the will of God prevailed and in spite of all entreaties and protests, they took up the Cross. Both had received the crown of glory in Heaven.

I walked from room to room and, as the guide was not talking about Paul Mary but about the Longford family tree, I timidly asked him to show me Paul Mary's portrait, for I had expected to find a huge one in a hallowed place. But all I encountered was a blank look, and then he said, 'Ah, yes, there is a picture of him somewhere in the next room, I think.' Finally, a small picture was produced. I now have a great devotion to, and belief in, the Blessed Paul Mary Pakenham.

Summer Days

Summer had come to Coolamber and the central heating was turned off until the autumn. Leisure hours were now spent mostly out of doors, or perhaps in the airy recreation room where a few sedate students congregated to sew, read or gossip. The soft June air and warm sun brought colour to our pale cheeks. The students' faces, arms and legs grew brown and all life bloomed, blossomed and improved. Then one day a storm broke like a monsoon with torrents of rain, thunder and lightning. Fortunately, no damage was done and three days later the sun shone down anew and the students were sprawling in the grass again, joking and laughing as if the skies had always been blue and would always remain so.

One day in July Uncle K arrived with nets, tennis rackets, putters and golf balls for clock golf. When I was in hospital I had become an expert clock golfer and I had made a hole in one three times, though not on the same day. Then I had come second in the clock-golf hospital championship. So I enthused over the golf, while others were keen on tennis and yet others wanted nothing but croquet. We all thanked Uncle K as he and Sweet William were trimming and flagging the different courses. He became more popular than ever with us, if that were possible. Now we had regular games to keep us outside, the rhythmic regular exercise necessary to develop and strengthen flabby muscles and quicken our heartbeats. In the evenings, tired from work or play, we would sit and watch television or maybe read or sew.

During that summer term Coolamber proposed to give a concert at the next meeting of the ICA. Pet was to coach all talent. I offered a sketch I had written myself, but it was considered too long. The programme was to consist of short musical items. At last, Pet got all her talent marshalled into order and we royally entertained our visitors. Rose danced a hornpipe in irons. A fortnight later we were pleased to hear that the doctor had given her permission to leave off the irons altogether; but that is another story, Rose's story. (This doctor was the local practitioner, a charming man with impeccable professional manners. Dr S.R. had great faith in God and in humanity. He advocated the early removal of crutches, irons and supports, and his advice and treatments were invariably beneficial.)

The concert was a success and the students all charmed the ICA visitors with their singing, dancing and recitations. Tea was served, as was usual after all ICA meetings. The President allowed ICA members to invite students they had met to visit them at weekends. I received several such invitations and so passed many an agreeable afternoon. Our President was always most appreciative of these invitations and always reminded us to write a note of thanks afterwards.

Meanwhile, cookery lectures went on regularly: ginger-bread, German slices, Eccles cakes, crème Chantilly. Each recipe was taught and demonstrated by Miss Honey. We cooked and baked and later on we enjoyed what we had made at tea or supper. We learned the culinary arts, the repertoire of French written menus, à la this and à la that, and as much cookery as we could cram into a year's training.

Students at Coolamber took a great natural pride in their appearance. New hats were bought frequently and new shoes and dresses. The summer days seemed to fly by whenever there was a dance. After supper there was a frenzy of pow-dering, mascara-ing, eye-shadowing and lipsticking. There was a swapping of earrings or headbands or rings. Many students had found admirers in Longford, much to the dismay of home sweethearts, I should imagine.

Last Days at Coolamber

By July we were making redcurrant and blackcurrant jelly. Out on the washing line in the yard jelly bags were to be seen floating in the breeze. The stores of preserves were increasing, the barley was ripening, the lovely crimson and green rhubarb glowed in the soil, cauliflowers, onions, leeks and lettuces pushed their way up to add to the show of colour. Little flags with the name of the herb or vegetable stood at the head of each neat drill. Just inside the white garden gate was lavender and I often picked a sprig or two to scent my clothes. The black grapes would be plentiful in September, judging by what they looked like now, and the peaches would soon be ripe, while the tomatoes were steadily climbing and getting bigger. The geranium pots, as usual, brightened up the glass-houses.

My last term was almost over. It was August, my course was nearly finished and employment was the immediate problem. I savoured my last month in Coolamber. I was sorry to be leaving yet happy. I had benefited enormously from the experience and the excellent tuition. I had enjoyed the companionship of the other students and the general sociability.

Now that I had decided to leave, some of the girls who were staying on to specialise in further studies would say to me, 'Joan, it is well for you, you will be going soon.'

'You will never feel a few months passing. Be happy while you can and pray for employment,' I would reply.

Then a close friend would say, 'What will I do without you?'

I would laugh and say, 'You will forget all about me eventually; but please answer my letters – I'll be looking forward to news of Coolamber.'

Uncle K came down from headquarters every week now to

interview students, to supervise agricultural innovations and to check accounting and finance. When the hay-making began, Uncle K could be seen with the hay-makers, gathering up the hay energetically. Then he would stop for a rest, and laugh and talk cheerfully with us. If we were drinking orange squash, he also would drink a glass or two. He would talk shop on these occasions, forecasting the weather, the yield of crops and other farming matters. Uncle K was a good conversationalist when the occasion arose, but primarily he was a man of action and few words. His silence was not the embarrassing type, but rather a thoughtful, reflective silence, as if he were thinking about you and might actually do something about it. We felt he understood us and that he knew our needs. He understood the problems facing handicapped people, and perhaps this was because he himself had been ill in hospital for a time. He understood our difficulties: starting a new job, with no experience, some handicaps perhaps, and no friends.

I must also pay tribute here to our employment officer, the woman who knew each individual student's medical history and who found suitable employment for us. She was a sister of Seán McCurtain, a great Irishman. She was also a dedicated and untiring worker in the cause of rehabilitation. At my interview she talked to me earnestly and questioned me gently in a few personal matters. I rather shamefacedly confessed that up to then I had sold only four or five raffle tickets and a box of flags on Flag Day. Imagine my surprise at the store she set by this puny effort of mine to aid Rehabilitation. She was most gracious and kind, and thanked me as if I had organised a *fleadh* or something. This praise and confidence in me spurred me on to greater efforts. After that I sold tickets whenever I could and joined the Rehabilitation Pools myself.

Later on in August the awaited news came. Employment

had been secured for me but first I had to be interviewed by my future employer. My recommendations were excellent and I found no difficulty in accepting the terms offered. I took an immediate liking to my employer, both of us were satisfied and I was offered the job. I was going to a seaside suburban area and I was delighted as I loved the sea. I had a week to prepare and to say goodbye to Coolamber. I would never forget this place, which made liberty a reality for me.

Last Words

When I was in school, and afterwards, we had a Past Pupils' Union, and I hope Coolamber will have time one day to in-augurate something similar for its past students. It would be nice to visit annually and see the improvements there. Today, it is changing, expanding. Every day old unused stables and out-buildings are being demolished, and lecture rooms, dairies and craft rooms are taking their place. Improvements are always being made at Coolamber. The material is there, and a ready warm sympathy for disabled people. Visitors are always welcome and are often surprised the modern conveniences there. The building may look old and venerable on the outside, but on the inside it is a modern college of industry and endeavour. A picture of the Sacred Heart that hangs inside, promises help in this world as well as happiness in the next. The library is and was a great blessing. No subscription is demanded and students desirous of knowledge, or lovers of lit-erature, can always find an abundant supply of reading matter there. From time to time donors hand in new books, so there is always something interesting to read on a wet evening. There are books on bee-keeping, poultry, horticulture, agriculture, religion, war and peace. The arts and crafts section is very popular with the students.

Coolamber makes useful citizens of people and students who come to love Coolamber will leave it as if they have left a very dear friend behind, one who loves wisely and then sends its children away to make good of their lives. I wonder do the patrons and benefactors of Rehabilitation realise, as I do, how much health and happiness it is in their power to give to the handicapped and the disabled. When they take on a new student it can signal a new lease of life for her. Setbacks recede at Coolamber, and optimism and success prevail. The subscribers to the Pools, the buyers of raffle tickets, the whist drives all help to rehabilitate patients who have spent a long spell in hospitals and give them a fresh start in life. There were girls at Coolamber in my day who knew no other life but hospital life. Some would have had nothing to look forward to other than a long-term hospital bed or returning home to spend the rest of their life as an invalid. I have seen crutches and irons taken off in Coolamber for good – and is that not a miracle?

Some day, please God, Coolamber will rehabilitate vast numbers that otherwise would have no chance of employment. This project surely has God's blessing: 'As long as you did it to these, the least of My brethren, you did it to Me.'

Part Two

The Housekeeper

Introduction*

When I returned to the world to earn my living I had no home, no relations to care for me or advise me. I was alone with my thoughts and with my past. I could not easily explain to people – especially those I wished to become friends with – where I had been and why. So I decided to write a book. I described how I had been locked away for almost twenty years, and that only now, in middle age, had I returned to the world again.

Many aspects of the world that I had known, worked and played in were changed, for the better occasionally and sometimes for the worse. The whole tempo of life had accelerated. The public seemed insatiable for change, for speed. Jumbo jets were streaking across continents in a few hours, communications were at a new level of sophistication. Television was the most popular medium; now one half of the world could see what the other half was doing. Natural disasters seemed more terrible now that the reporting of them was accompanied by pictures on 'live' television. In my younger days news was mostly 'canned', as the Americans say, recorded, photographed or filmed through the channels of newspaper, radio and newsreel. By contrast, the death of President John F. Kennedy was seen by millions instantly, as it happened, on television, just as his brother Robert's assassination five years later was also immediately communicated to the world. Television nightly showed small nations and territories in rebellion, demanding their human and civil rights. All this had come about within the two decades I had been shut away. And now here I was, confident that, with my new-found freedom, every other blessing would follow; and if happiness did not come to me, at least I was free to pursue it.

3 May 1974

* Names of persons and some places have been changed to preserve anonymity.

My First Job

After I had managed to escape from 'you know where', the Committee sent me to a domestic science rehabilitation school called Coolamber Manor in County Longford. I remained there for a year. The course was designed to prepare its students for the hard workaday world. We were given the option of training for a range of jobs: cooks, confectioners, poultry keepers, dairymaids and housekeepers. I chose the last of these. When the year ended, I graduated with honours in Domestic Economy, in both theory and practical tests. I attributed this excellence to my maturity and a sangfroid that was cultivated rather than inherited.

While I was still at Coolamber, the principal arranged my first employment. A lady doctor, a gynaecologist, had approached her seeking a cook-housekeeper. She was looking for a sensible, reliable, mature person and, when she heard of my capabilities, she said without more ado that I was just the right person for her. So it was arranged that I should take on the duties of housekeeper at her residence a week after the interview.

So, in the month of August in the optimistic 1960s, I set out by train and bicycle. The house was on a hill, and I was tired and dusty when I arrived after a long journey. The doctor was expecting me. She gave me refreshments in the kitchen, then conducted me on a tour of the house and briefed me on my various tasks. These were twofold: domestic and in the surgery. From 7 a.m. to 2 p.m. my work included washing and ironing of clothes and linen, fire-setting and bed-making. (My employer was unmarried and lived alone.) There was much work with mop, pail and carpet-sweeper. (There was no Hoover.) As for cooking, I learned that the doctor liked underdone grilled steak, grilled brill on Fridays and soup with a 'bite' to it, which meant having diced vegetables in it. She was very fond of soup. My surgery duties commenced at 2 p.m. The doctor saw her patients in the surgery. I sat in the kitchen and each time the bell rang I opened the front door and ushered the patient into the doctor's presence. Usually I had to work seventy-five to eighty hours a week. I was allowed two afternoons off each week from 3 p.m. However, I was not really free on those afternoons because I was always worried about the time, for I had to return in time to prepare the fires for the morning, remove the ashes, take in fuel, and do any other chore that needed my attention. These hours were too long, and the wages for domestics were unrealistically low – £3 per week.

While the doctor was in the surgery, her gardener, John, would take advantage of her absence and come into the kitchen for a cup of tea. One day, after we had been acquainted for just a week, he told me ardently that he could no longer suppress his love for me. I discouraged him then and on five or six other occasions, but finally, one afternoon when I was bored and idle, I allowed him to put his arm around my waist. However, he was too impetuous for me. I just wanted to be friends – but he refused to be deterred. He kept asking me for a date and one day, somewhat to my own surprise, I agreed to meet him under the lamp-post opposite the local cinema on my next half-day off, five days later.

In the meantime he became very communicative and made many disclosures about our employer, one of which was that no housekeeper had ever stayed with her for more than a month. I was very perturbed to hear this and pressed him for further details. Naturally, he was anxious to please me, so he went on to tell me that he had dated all my predecessors and that they had all been of the one mind, and he himself had agreed, that doctors, as such, were narrow-minded, and that working for one was no position for a girl with high spirits and a normal appetite. Were it not for him, he said, they would all have left after a few days, but as it was they put up with the doctor's exacting ways for his sake.

At this point I decided not to meet him on my half-day after all. I was not really attracted to him; and also he had suggested going for a *walk* instead of taking a seat at the cinema opposite. I thought I would wait for true love, for true love would not have tried to walk me off my feet after a hard day's work. Furthermore, I would not cheapen myself and go walking with the first man who asked me. So I sent word to him, via the milkman, who incidentally was related to him, that due to circumstances beyond my control I could not keep our appointment. Unfortunately he had already, indiscreetly and impetuously, recounted exaggerated details of his wooing and of the pending date with me to his friends and neighbours, who in due course passed it on to my employer, the gynaecologist. Up to this point she had expressed satisfaction with my work. As a good housekeeper I was invaluable to her, and it was important to her to retain me in her service for a decent length of time, especially as her former housekeepers had left regularly and her monthly notice for a replacement appeared just as regularly in the Situations Vacant column of the local paper, not to mention the nationals. It was always her policy to keep her housekeeper and her equally invaluable gardener at a distance from each other, for fear of a joint walk-out to connubial bliss.

However, a week later the storm broke. 'Hanna,' she said sharply. 'Is it true that you and my gardener are carrying on in the shed? I can't have this sort of gossip.' I was temporarily speechless. Had she heard his amorous advances from outside the shed, when she went out to the clothes line for her nylons perhaps, or was it just idle gossip? I was annoyed as I had just rejected him via the milkman, but I decided to confide the truth to her anyway, woman to woman. I explained that I had agreed to meet him for a date but on reflection had not done so, for personal reasons.

I began my explanation, but she had preconceived ideas about housekeepers and gardeners, and she interrupted me, speaking severely: 'I don't want excuses. You may take a week's notice, Hanna. I shall take a girl from the convent, and you may look for other employment.' Today, with more experience, I know that gardeners are more valuable to gynaecologists than housekeepers, in Ireland anyway. Anyhow, I accepted her rebuke with apparent meekness, but in a strange way I was actually relieved to be free from her constraints, and I agreed to find alternative employment.

The Next Step

I read the Situations Vacant that evening and the next day I went to see three prospective employers. I asked a relative who had been an employment officer which job I should accept. He firmly denounced all the ladies I had met, having formed an unfavourable impression of them as being immoral and scandalous. He also told me that housekeepers had complained to him of not being paid. His wife agreed with him. She also spoke of scandal, but I knew that she was a member of the same sodality as the gynaecologist and that she was embarrassed by my employment there. I believed what they said, but they had their own motives, I realise now, as I was in their view a despicable common domestic, while all their family were social aspirants. Anyhow, my relative spoke with prejudicial despair of my ever finding employment in Ireland, especially in his area. He strongly advised me to go to a visiting agency that was in the town to recruit girls for the awaiting emigrant ships destined for the faraway ports of Scotland, England and America.

I know I should have persevered, but I had a week's notice and there were only four days left before the convent girl arrived to replace me. I was resistant to going abroad, but he insisted that it was my only prospect and added that abroad I would have anonymity and more prosperous conditions. I did not see his logic, for I had never sought anonymity or prosperity. I would have been content with a modicum of happiness and a stable livelihood. I realised then that nobody cared about what happened to me. All they wanted was to banish me again.

The agency had rented a suite of luxurious rooms in a well-known hotel. I was tranquillised by plush carpets and the amber concealed lighting. I entered the pre-interview apartment five storeys up. The agent was as deluxe as the atmosphere. You would think it was I who was doing her the favour. I told her of my qualifications, stating that it was the opinion of the various people that I had been of service to that I was an excellent cook-housekeeper. She seemed impressed and replied in a very friendly and open manner. A friend of her own family and of her personal acquaintance lived with his wife and grown-up family in a beautiful house near London. She said he was of Irish nationality and a millionaire. He owned about fifty pubs, but, she stressed, he needed a cook-housekeeper for his country house where the family lived. Naturally, when I heard of the pubs I mentioned that I had some experience of pubs, because my family had owned and run one in Athlone before my father died, and that I would really prefer a position in one of the millionaire's bars. She reminded me that it was a cook-housekeeper he needed, not a barmaid. She said that if I wanted the position she would write to him on my behalf and personally recommend me. Visions of sociable occasions and cosmopolitan repartee in the convivial atmosphere of a bar faded and I realised she was still talking, explaining that cook-housekeepers were a rare commodity indeed, almost impossible to procure, and that she would advise me to accept, as the family was typically Irish – kind, patient, religious – and that they would treat me as one of the family. So then I thought that, as I was over a barrel and had only three days left of my notice until the convent girl arrived, I should accept her offer. I gave the necessary particulars, filled in the forms, obtained instructions as to the particulars of destination, travel routes, etc., and she said that my fare would be refunded on arrival.

I left the agency wondering just what I had got myself into. I was somewhat elated though at having obtained employment at two pounds a week more than my present weekly wage. I returned then to the demesne of the gynaecologist. I looked at the brass plate outside as I entered and felt relieved that I would not have to polish that monstrosity again at 7 a.m. each morning, Sundays excepted. The doctor greeted me with concern.

'Hanna, I hope you are doing something about another position.'

I tartly informed her that I had obtained a position of trust with a multimillionaire yeast baron in greater London. She was piqued and pressed me for more information, but I would discuss it no further. I reminded her that I should require a reference from her, backing up the reference from the principal of the domestic science rehabilitation school, that I was of good character and a good cook. Her reference read as follows:

Miss Greally is honest, sober and a good cook. If you require further information you may write or phone.

70

Fortunately, long-distance phone calls are expensive from London, even for millionaires, but I need not have worried, for, in the permissive society of swinging London that I came to, her garbled and narrow-minded account of my 'affair' with her gardener would be considered an intrusion into privacy and would not have cut much ice.

I then prepared to emigrate. I had saved £20, so I went shopping the next day after lunch. I wanted to try and look 'with it' for my travel to fashionable London. The clothes I had were shabby and too large, mostly Aunty's cast-offs. I had bought a new raincoat at a sale some weeks previously, but my coat was very old, for Aunty herself had worn it for five years and I had worn it for fifteen. I bought a pale green coat for £2. It also was second-hand, but it had been dry cleaned and looked as good as new. It was absolute luxury to me for, unlike Aunty's, it fitted me perfectly, showing off my waist, and it acted on me like a tonic, renewing my drooping spirits. I had a bicycle I had purchased from my fifteen-shillings-a-week pocket money at Coolamber. It had cost me £5 in all, £1 deposit and five shillings per week. I had completed the payments and now it was my own. I could not take it with me, so I decided to offer it to my relative for £5. His teenage schoolboy son did not have a bicycle, so I knew he would buy it for him, as it was going cheap. Next, I bought new shoes with Cuban heels and pointed toes, in contrast to the institutional ones I was still wearing. Finally, I bought a new corset and gossamer lingerie. Afterwards I found I had £5 left and my relative gave me a further £5 for the bicycle. I calculated then that I had enough for my fare (which would be refunded) and a few pounds left over for travelling expenses. As I counted the remaining notes I felt rich and secure, God help my ignorance, and I looked forward with naive anticipation to my future life with the millionaire and his Irish family.

The gynaecologist gave me a medal of Pope Paul when I was leaving and reminded me that, were it not for my indiscretion with the gardener, I would not have needed to look elsewhere for employment.

The Emigrant Ship

Long ago, or fadó, as we say in Ireland, there was an infamous emigrant ship. This was a ship that, unknown to me, awaited my arrival. I sailed in it from Dublin to Holyhead, and thence to 'Old Smoky', as my ancient uncle living in London still calls the city of his exile to this day. I wrote to this uncle saying I was on my way. I had one case with me and nobody at Dún Laoghaire to bid me farewell as I began the first stages of my long exile. So with my suitcase in one hand and my handbag in the other I queued up with the other travellers, waiting for the gangway to be declared open. The ship was called *Maud*. It was December and a gale was lashing the pier. In the queue I was between two men and they spoke to each other across my shoulder.

'If I knew it was the auld *Maud* I would have cancelled my bookin',' one said in a dismal tone.

'Why's that, Mick?' asked the other, completely ignoring me, the in-between.

He answered, shouting against the wind, 'Well, don't you know, she is flat-bottomed, and an ex-cattle boat. Everybody gets sick on her.'

'Oh Lord,' said the other, 'I'll never survive this night. I'll never forget the last time I went on the *Maud*. I wish I had known.'

'Nobody knew. Repairs to the *Prince* at the last moment, so they made the switch.'

The first man made a dreadful gulping sound, as if he had taken salts. I did not understand what all the fuss was about; then I learned that flat-bottomed boats are not suitable for the transport of humans. Well, flat-bottomed or round-bottomed, I thought, I cannot cancel my trip, as I am expected at Euston in the morning. I warn anybody who wishes to arrive in England healthy and steady never to go on a boat with a flat bottom called *Maud*, because it was awful. I travelled third class of course and I descended to a large cabin like a bunkhouse in *Maud*'s flat bottom. As I entered, the stewardess handed me one of those paper bags that are provided at sea. I chose a floor bunk, and the bunks, about thirty or forty of them, were in tiers of three. I put my case underneath and lay on it fully clothed (as others were), the paper bag clutched in my hand. There was noise, light and talk everywhere, not to mention the awful sound of engines. To further add to my discomfort, a number of hippies kept entering and leaving the cabin, putting their big feet in my face on the way up and down to their higher bunks. I know now that they were hippies, for they had long straggly hair and wore rough sheepskin jackets and imitation-fur garments. I was puzzled by one, in spite of my agony. He had what I thought was a real cat's tail dangling from his buckled leather belt. It was striped, a tiger cat's.

There was a storm and the ship heaved and waltzed and lurched dreadfully, and the engine purred and reared alternatively. I called out once that I was dying and I asked one calm and robust-looking lady for a drink. She was sitting on the only chair, near the open door, playing patience on a table. I asked her if she could get me soda water, or brandy, or anything.

'Anything,' I repeated, as she bent over me. 'Anything to relieve me in my last moments.' The patience lady returned with soda water. I paid her, and sipped it. My teeth were chattering, although the bunk-house was stifling. There was a fog of light, noise and moving people. Dust kept falling into my eyes from above, and due to this irritation I could not keep my eyes open for long. Eventually, I staggered out to the toilet, but I had to retreat as it was dangerously slippery. Travellers were queuing up to get sick, which was the cause of the dangerous condition of the floor. I tottered back, unrelieved, to the claustrophobia of the cabin again, crawled into my bunk, and suffered the rest of the journey with silent Irish heroism until we landed.

The next ordeal was the Customs. Had I anything to declare? A handsome bearded man bent over my open case and fingered my gossamer lingerie.

'Nothing, my Lord,' I answered.

I was allowed to pass and so I set foot again on English soil after thirty years' absence. Then it had been what you might call a mercy trip, for I had gone over during the Blitz as a Probationer Nurse. After Customs there was another queue, this time for the Holyhead-to-London train. It was dark and raining when I boarded the express, but six hours later, when I arrived at Euston Station in London, it was a typically cold December morning, dry and bright.

The Shagalls

I stood on the platform at Euston, lonely and uncertain what to do amidst all the bustling rush and noise. Then an attractive woman in her thirties approached me. She asked me my name and introduced herself as Breege, Mr Shagall's private secretary. As we chatted about the journey and the weather I learned that she was also an executive and shareholder in the millionaire brewing enterprise of Shagall & Heorna. Their selling motto was 'Drink Shagall, Drink Heorna, Drink your troubles away.' Breege mentioned that their advertising executive had thought out this slogan for their television campaign; I gathered that this one sentence had cost the firm 5,000 smackers. She had her car parked outside the station and, greetings and introductions over, she escorted me with my case to the car. The Shagalls' house was called 'Beart' and it was twenty minutes from London, or one hour by car, due to the density of the traffic. I did not speak much, as I was tired from travelling and the effects of the sea voyage had not yet worn off. Instead, I listened as intelligently as I could and inserted yes, no and maybe at suitable intervals. She startled me once by referring to a puma that had escaped from Chessington Zoo and had been sighted in the Shagall area. I had never seen a puma. The cars were flying past us at seventy miles an hour. I thought of the remote country parts of Ireland, where buses were scarce and travelled at thirty miles an hour, where trains puffed along at twenty and I usually cycled, pedalling furiously, to my various destinations at a meagre ten.

We were deep in the country now. Breege slowed down and I came back from dreaming.

I spoke: 'I see Mr Shagall's beverages are displayed on the buses,' I said, and she replied that he owned fifty pubs and that 'advertising paid'. We turned into an avenue of pine trees and, by the time we arrived at the front door, I knew that he had two sons and a wife and liked everything Irish. He had relatives in the Cork area and they posted to him each week, in the following order of priority:

> One pig's head (registered)
> Two pig's cheeks (registered)
> Christmas, Easter and Thanksgiving turkeys (unregistered)

Holy water, poteen and Irish newspapers (unregistered)
as well as many other exclusive items only obtainable
from the 'auld sod'.

The house was surprisingly small. I had expected a palace. But of course it was exclusive and detached, which in England signifies that you have the 'lolly'. Anne Boleyn must have lived in this part of the country, for there was the Anne Boleyn Bridle Walk nearby and in the village there was a shop called Anne Boleyn's Pantry. I had tea and pastries there once.

We were now near the front door. There was a tennis court bordered by trees, which looked neglected and had squirrels playing on it. I learned later that squirrels were prolific in that area. I was given two warnings on my first day. The first was about the puma, which was black, and which people nearby had reported seeing. The second was not to be startled if I heard noise on the roof at night, for it was only squirrels scampering about.

We got out of the car and Breege showed me the garden. There was a glass-house which had a basin of onions or bulbs inside on a high bench. Breege told me that Mr Shagall had sowed a patch of Irish wheat in the back garden. It looked weedy to my mind, more like wilted pampas grass, but then it was not the season for wheat.

Breege and I then went inside, where I was introduced to Mrs Shagall and the younger son, Seán. He was forty-two. Mrs Shagall was sixty, a plump, smiling, plain woman, and obviously Irish. She was kind-hearted and very motherly, neither drank nor smoked, and lived solely for her husband and sons. She was completely subservient to Mr Shagall. All life to her revolved around Mr Shagall, whether he was in bed or up. Mrs Shagall said her husband was 'indisposed', and then Seán, who acted as valet to his father, said that Mr Shagall would interview me later, but in his bedroom. Whenever Mr Shagall wanted anybody or anything he knocked three times on the floor with a huge shillelagh and Seán ran up to minister to his needs.

Mrs Shagall poured tea for Breege, Seán and myself. Soon, we heard three loud bangs on the ceiling and Mrs Shagall said: 'He wants to know if you have arrived. I expect he will call you up soon. Breege, will you show Hanna her room, and I will go up and see if he is ready.'

Breege and I went up to my room. I was so tired I could have slept then, for I had not slept for two nights and the travel by boat and train had fatigued me considerably. I unpacked. Contrary to what I had expected, the room was very tiny, box-like, but it was tastefully furnished with suitable boudoir pieces, and the one bathroom and toilet was beside it at right angles and facing the stairs. This toilet caused me great annoyance during my stay there, for Seán and Seamus, who were hard drinkers, frequented it at half-hourly intervals during the night. Night for them started when they returned from the pub at midnight or so, and they usually slept from about 4 a.m. after which the water-gushing ceased.

Seamus, the elder son, had returned from America some months before I came. He had been a student of entymology there and had a highly embossed degree certificate hanging on the wall of his bedroom. Seamus was handsome. He looked like the film star Clark Gable and he had the same sort of moustache. Breege was in love with Seamus even before he went to America. Seamus was not in love with her, I noticed, but Seán *was* in love with Breege. Seán was the younger son, valet and relief cook, which must have been an affront to Breege. It was difficult at first to sort out the conflicts, the undercurrents, but I knew who loved whom as soon as they sat down to television. The pattern of preference for certain chairs or couches changed and what they avoided as uncomfortable one day, they endured for love's sake the next. Take one night of 'telly'. Breege sat on the couch beside Seamus and throughout the show looked adoringly at his profile instead of at the television. (Mrs Shagall knitted mittens for Mr Shagall during the show and seemed unaware of any of this.) Seán sat on the other side of Breege and tried to draw her attention to him by criticising the show. When he talked loudly Seamus would look disturbed; then Seán would speak in a whisper and Breege would become uncomfortable and move to an armchair. The manoeuvres and strategies of love were painfully obvious. Seamus really was impervious to Breege's seductions; all he cared about was gin and insects.

I had unpacked and washed and tidied myself when Breege knocked on my bedroom door. She said she would take me to meet Mr Shagall. We came to a door further down the red-carpeted landing. I felt nervous, as I had never met a millionaire before. When we knocked, an unmistakeable Irish accent boomed out, 'Come in. Come in.' We entered respect-fully. Mr Shagall was in bed. He looked strong and healthy for his seventy years. I stood with Breege at the foot of his large four-poster bed. His voice boomed again. He had a remark-ably strong voice for his age.

'Come in, child.'

He smiled through a great beard, grey and wavy and long, just like the one on my statue of St Patrick. The *Financial Times* was scattered all over the bed. There were two telephones on bedside tables, one on his right and one on his left. A nocturnal convenience was visible under the bed. When I came in, he left down on the bed a sheet of paper covered with figures. By the size of the columns I could see he had been calculating not in hundreds, but in thousands.

Seán stood respectfully by his father's bed. Mr Shagall shook hands with me and, as is the custom in Ireland, I responded warmly. Seán put a seat beside the bed and Mr Shagall invited me to sit down and tell him all about what part of Ireland I came from and was this my first time in England. Before I left his bedroom, he asked me if I liked pig's head, bacon and cabbage, porridge and wholemeal homemade brown bread. I assured him I loved them, and that I was expert at cooking those specific dishes. He said he liked a boiled egg for breakfast, but it was not to be cooked one second beyond four minutes. I assured him that I had a minute hand on my watch and I would see to it that the egg was boiled exactly. The phone rang just then beside him and Seán ushered me out into the hall, where I encountered Breege, who took me to the kitchen and told me my duties. The set-up was as follows. Seán stoked the boiler. Seán attended to his father and took up all his meals. I noticed Seán never went to his father's pubs on business, as his brother Seamus did. Seán went to pubs for pleasure. Seamus combined both.

Shawneen, whom I was yet to meet, was a sort of daily handyman who lived out. He was a hunchback, who came five or six days a week and returned home each evening. Shawneen chopped wood for the boiler and fires, tidied the garden and had 'hotel experience'. He told me that I had but to command him and he would obey. I put this to the test some days later, and also his 'hotel experience'. Seamus arrived back from London with an Irish turkey, an Irish ham, a case of Irish whiskey, a case of gin and three cases of tonic water. This supply for home consumption was delivered every Friday by the firm's private van. Mr Shagall believed in having plenty of his own stock available. (I was told via Breege that I could drink as much tonic water as I cared for, but advised that, as good cooks were better off sober, the rest of the stuff was taboo. I never drank a glass of water while there; it was tonic,

tonic, tonic all the time. I don't know if tonic water was the cause, but I had twelve teeth extracted while I was with the Shagalls.)

It was almost Christmas week and Mrs Shagall said they would have the turkey, goose and ham cooked that Sunday and that a few guests would call. I was unprepared for this setback, for the turkey was feathered and whole, inside and out, as was the goose. I said to Breege that it was rather a lot, and that I usually cooked oven-ready fowl. I was putting the ham in to cook at the time. She said: 'Not to worry,' she said, 'Shawneen will help you. He spent years at it in the hotels.'

Shawneen seemed to be the solution to everybody's emergency there. He arrived at 10 a.m. He was small and he had a definite hump in his back, but he was good-tempered and apparently did not think about his disability. He probably had grown used to it, for when I had known him only a week he tried to make a date with me. I said I had toothache and he accepted this and subsequent excuses and refusals perfectly cheerfully.

My first interview with him was one of extreme urgency, for a turkey and goose had to be plucked, cleaned and oven-prepared for the Shagall family's Sunday lunch and dinner. Breege left us alone in a little ante-chamber off the kitchen. I invited Shawneen to sit down and offered him tea. He declined and said that he had to take a case of gin and whiskey to the respective rooms of Seán and Seamus and that later on he would have a drink there. I got down to domestic business.

'Can you prepare a turkey and goose for me tomorrow? I believe you have hotel experience, Shawneen?'

That chore was negligible as far as he was concerned.

'Take them out to the tool shed tomorrow, and we'll do them there,' he said.

I slept well that night, confident that Shawneen would take care of the birds.

Next morning, we plucked and cleaned out the fowl on a tree stump in the shed. I asked Shawneen to help me draw the sinews of the turkey, but he said he had never drawn the sinews, that he left them in. I explained that all we had to do was insert a knitting needle (as I had been shown in the domestic science college). Shawneen grinned disinterestedly. I reminded him of his offer to help and asked him to hold the turkey down on the tree stump and pull one way while I pulled the other way, in order to draw the sinews. We wrestled for an hour with the dead bird, but unfortunately every sinew broke when half-drawn. Shawneen considered the problem and the bird enigmatically. I considered whether to leave the remainder of the sinews in or whether to cut off the two sinews I had extracted. I decided to explain to Mrs Shagall and Breege that the sinews refused to be drawn. All that could decently be done now was to cut off the torn sinews and she would see that the legs were given to somebody who would not know the difference. Shawneen spoke at last.

'Hanna, we could cut off the legs and put them in with the stock.'

I glared at him, for he was supposed to be experienced, and in *hotels*, too. Then I relented, when I thought how he had helped me, and I replied gently, 'There is no point in mutilating it any further, Shawneen, it's not your fault or mine. We will just cut the broken sinews off,' and I suited the action to the word and Shawneen held the turkey while I snipped with the pruning scissors.

Mrs Shagall or Breege must have asked Mr Shagall's advice about the sinews, as the following incident proves. That same evening as I was laying the dining-room table, Mr Shagall beckoned me to a fireside armchair. I sat there wondering nervously if there was a problem. He was six-foot-three or four and he towered above me on the hearth, his back to the fire. He seemed preoccupied, like a man with a problem, while at the same time trying to give his attention to me. He spoke portentously, like a teacher who had a cane hidden behind his back.

'What's this I hear, Hanna, about you not able to draw the sinews of the turkey? Didn't your mother show you how to do it when you were in Ireland?' His incredulous tone made me feel small and guilty, as if I had committed some crime with the unfortunate turkey. 'Did she not?' he asked again.

'No, sir, we never had turkey at home, never. We were too poor, we just had rabbits.'

I looked up at him nervously, to see if he accepted my explanation, and I thought he looked disgusted at the mention of rabbits, but all he said was 'Shawneen ought to be able to draw sinews, he claims to be at it for twenty years in hotel kitchens.' I was about to ask him who had drawn the sinews before I came but I thought better of it, and so I left him, again with that preoccupied look on his face.

Well, I can't blame Shawneen for the goose anyhow for I had cleaned it out, after he plucked it. I did not discover the dreadful mistake I had made until after lunch, which was fortunate. Even when I stuffed it I never remarked it. You see, a goose is so fat that anybody might make the same mistake. I discovered what I had done only after the goose had been carved and partially eaten by the family. The carcass was sent out to me by Seán. I ate some of it with vegetables. Later on, as I broke up the carcass to put it in the stock pot, I was amazed to find tightly lodged in its neck, or craw, a pouch of oats. I murmured a prayer of thanks that the oats had not spilled out when the goose was on the family table at lunch. This time I did not tell anyone, for, as the saying goes, what you don't know, won't worry you, or even out of sight, out of mind. Now mark this, you who may hold me responsible for the state of that goose, geese are very secretive fowl and store their hoard as cleverly and secretly as a human miser.

Shortly after that dinner Breege had some sort of a tiff with Seán and refused to massage his chest. Seán thought he had asthma and Breege sometimes used to massage his chest and apply an embrocation. She hated the job because she said his chest was hairy. So when he asked me to massage him I felt sorry for him and did so. I agreed with Breege then, for it was a messy job, the hair was too dense and the embrocation could not adhere to the chest. As I rubbed I said, 'Sean, have you ever tried inhalations?' and he never asked me again.

I remained with the Shagalls for about six months. About a month before I left, Seamus' engagement was announced in *The Times*. His fiancée was an actress in a popular musical then showing in the West End. She visited the Shagalls once while I was there, and I was upset for two reasons. I could not find the coffee spoons that evening and I quietly apologised to her for using the egg spoons. 'Madam, I cannot find the Apostle spoons.'

She was quite nice about it and laughingly replied, 'Never mind, darling. The Irish never think of the Apostles. Now, if they were called St Patrick's spoons or St Anthony's spoons, they would be all over the show.'

Breege was not there that night. She had an important appointment, she said, but I knew that her heart was broken over Seamus' engagement. Afterwards, the mystery of the missing spoons was solved. Seán had put them in the family safe – God knows why. His unrequited love for Breege made him do the most absurd things.

Well, you will wonder why I left after only six months there. I left for personal reasons, as I told Mr and Mrs Shagall. I wanted to work in London, I said, where I would see my uncle occasionally. I pretended he was in failing health and that, as he was single, he needed care while he was convalescing. My real reasons were: firstly, the squirrels were very noisy on the roof at night and I could not sleep. Secondly, the toilet flushed too often at night, possibly because of the gin. Thirdly, I wanted to meet the natives, the English people, for a change. So back to the papers I went and the Situations Vacant. I saw that a cook was wanted in a monastery, so I wrote and received a reply asking me to go to west London for an interview. I did this on my day off and I was accepted as cook to the community.

The Shagalls were sorry to lose me. They gave me a lovely reference stating that I was an excellent cook-housekeeper, and that I was diligent, sober, etc., and that I was leaving them for personal reasons of a family nature. The prior of the monastery was satisfied with my references and I arranged to go on a Saturday and take up residence at the housekeeper's apartment at the monastery. My new apartment was the top floor of a house that was once occupied by a mistress of some English monarch 300 years ago. The house was very old, but I did not care whether it was old or new. It was in a sequestered spot in London and, although in a monastery, at least I was in the heart of the metropolis where love and adventure might await me.

The Monastery

The monastery was situated in a quiet secluded area in London. I arrived there on a Saturday afternoon and I had until the following Monday to settle into my new apartment. This was to be my new home. It was situated in the monastery grounds, a few hundred yards from the kitchen where I would work. I had a sitting-room, a bedroom and a bathroom, on the top floor of a 300-year-old house. The time was spring. My window looked out on the monks' private graveyard. Pretty little snowdrops grew around and on the graves. I did not find graveyards depressing, for in the past I had spent a number of years in a bedroom quite near to one and I associated them with quiet and rest for those who had found peace at last. Father John, the kitchen monk, introduced me gradually to the dailies, who were married and worked there as chars and washers-up six days a week, and to the houseboys, of whom there were four. They worked on a rota system, two on and two off each day. They occupied the ground floor of the house in which I had my apartment. The houseboys were not really boys at all: the youngest was about forty.

There was a paved garden path from the house where we lived to the community kitchen where I worked. Three married women were employed as kitchen helps, and they washed and prepared large quantities of vegetables under my direction and did all the washing-up by hand. When they had finished their kitchen work they left on a tour of the entire monastery, sweeping, dusting and polishing as they went. They offered to 'do' my apartment but I said I would do it myself, as they had enough on their plates. The community dining-room was next to the kitchen, but had no entrance to it for it was forbidden territory for women. A large panel in the wall, which was called the grille, was the means by which I passed the food inside to the two serving monks. There was a sliding wooden door in the grille. Strict silence was observed inside during meals, except for one voice, that of the Reader, whose voice droned on throughout the meal. Occasionally, the reading was from the Bible, but more often it was the life of a saint – perhaps the saint whose feast day it was. I was told not to speak to the servers when I passed the food to them through the grille, as they would not answer, having taken a strict vow of silence. In fact, it was forbidden for me to address any cowled monk in the monastery, with one exception: Father John, the kitchen monk, the medium for communication for all lay staff. (The houseboys were excepted and were allowed to talk to some of the monks.) Father John had a dispensation to talk to me when necessary, to pay my wages and to listen to and comment on suggestions for menus, gastronomic improvements and so on.

On certain great feast days, big dinners were given to visiting ecclesiastics. I remember once discussing a menu with Father John for a distinguished visitor, Archbishop Heenan then, now His Eminence Cardinal Heenan. It was the principal feast day at the monastery and famous old boys of the monastery school were invited, as well as the Archbishop. We decided on melon with cherries, consommé, beef Tournedos, sprouts, carrots, creamed potatoes. The sweet was a problem, but we solved it eventually. Father John agreed it was just the thing – a Russian soufflé: the usual eggs and castor sugar base, though this time using two dozen eggs, and when the soufflé was almost ready we added large quantities of rum, which is the main ingredient of this recipe.

The dinner was a marvellous success. The Archbishop and the prior sent complimentary word to me through Father John, and afterwards, I remember, when all the dignitaries had left, Father John gave me an envelope with a £5 note inside and thanked me on behalf of the community for the wonderful feast they had all so enjoyed.

One of the monks, a venerable, kind old saint of a man, was very elderly, deaf and slow in his movements. He took an extra hour and a half to say his prayers and to say Mass. I did not know about this disability for a day or two, when he sent word to me with a houseboy to always keep his breakfast late and he would let me know when he arrived at the refectory, the name given to their dining-room behind the grille. One morning a houseboy came into the kitchen and said that Father Jerome was in the Refectory and to send out his breakfast to him. I thought it was rather early for him, as I had served only about half of the breakfasts so far. However, I immediately cooked his breakfast as he liked it: his rashers crispy and his egg 'sunny side up'. I knocked at the grille.

'Father Jerome's breakfast,' I said.

The serving monk did not speak as I passed the plate through with the rasher and egg on it. What I did not know then was that there were two Father Jeromes. There was a knock on the grille some time later, and when I opened it I heard a weak, tearful voice on the other side.

'Please, Father Jerome's breakfast.'

'Father Jerome has already had his breakfast,' I answered.

'I have not,' he replied tearfully. 'Somebody has taken it.'

I soothed him and said I would prepare another breakfast especially for him immediately, which I did. He waited inside, for when I opened the grille he took the plate from me himself, as everybody else had left, and thanked me in a joyful voice, like a child appeased. I remember another morning when I was about to go back to my apartment and a houseboy came into the kitchen and grabbed the half-gallon can of nut oil which was under the table. He unscrewed the cap, poured a quantity into the cup of his hand and proceeded to rub the nut oil vigorously into his thinning sandy hair. When I asked him what he thought he was doing, he replied, 'I do it regular. It's very good for my hair. It strengthens it.'

One monk of Irish nationality grew shamrock in a little plot in the garden. He told Father John to tell me that he would show me the plot where the shamrock was and that I could take some for St Patrick's Day. I went to see the plot some days after and sure enough it was real shamrock all right and not clover. So it was that the old fable about shamrocks refusing to grow anywhere but in Irish soil perished in my mind on that day in an English monastery garden. The old gardener monk,

Father Gregory, had also heard the fable, and had in fact believed it himself one time, he said.

'Yes, I know about that belief but here they are. They grew for me anyhow, and they have been here for years.'

All the monks were simple, kind, uncomplicated people and to see one alone and meditating would remind you of Gethsemane. I never saw them at recreation.

I cooked for the entire community, thirty monks, four houseboys, three dailies – who just took lunches and elevenses – and myself. The dailies did all the tedious chores, washing-up, etc., and all I had to do was cook and think out a variety of menus for each week. I also ordered supplies by phone. We bought all dry stores in bulk, and fresh meat and perishables were delivered daily. Milk was delivered but the monks grew their own vegetables. They made and distilled their own wine and a beautiful rare wine it was. Father John told me that it was made from a secret recipe that was hundreds of years old and exclusively owned by their community. Apple pie was a favourite of the community while I was cook. I usually served a large milk pudding, rice or tapioca, for lunch in a three- by four-foot pie dish, but in the evening for dinner at about 7 p.m. their favourite pie was apple pie. I made a huge one in a similar-sized dish and they loved it. No matter how much sugar I put in it, and castor sugar on top of it, they would always send back the sugar shakers to be refilled. They were very fond of sugar.

Father John told me that once he had been a barrister before he entered the monastery. He said he had found London life empty and superficial and had become a monk to find peace and happiness. The other monks I met were usually cowled and they all looked the same – a prayerful silent community, walking alone or in twos, heads bowed, eyes cast down in constant meditation. Life passed by there for me without incident, but it was very dull, even though I was used to dullness. Then one day Father John came into the kitchen with a letter from an elderly woman they had once employed as housekeeper before she married and left. She was a widow now and had written to Father John wanting to know if the community would take her on again, as an assistant housekeeper or in any domestic capacity at all. He asked me if I needed an assistant and I replied that it would be a good idea. On reflection later I thought that the application from the old housekeeper was an opportunity for me to seek new pastures. I really was not happy there, for I felt very lonely. I also felt sorry for the monks for, although I knew they had chosen the life, they always appeared miserable to me. They may have believed they were happy, but generally they expected happiness only in the next world. I did, too, but I wanted to find it in this world as well. 'The Kingdom of Heaven is within you,' says Christ. Happiness, the monks believed, was also within you, but I knew I would be happy within me only if I were home in Ireland. However, although the little Emerald Isle was my home, all of it, I had no parents with a house there to go back to.

So I came to a decision. First, I put an advertisement in the *London Advertiser* under 'Domestics'. I had decided to give a month's notice. The ex-housekeeper was due to arrive within a week, which would give her ample time to settle in again. I carefully worded my resignation to the prior, saying that I had received more suitable employment near my uncle's house in London. (Actually, anywhere in London was near Uncle Pete, with tube trains, etc.) I also said that I would stay on as long as necessary to show the ex-housekeeper any new developments that may have been introduced since her time. When I had sent the letter to the prior by the houseboy, I contacted Father John before Matins and told him that I had sent it. Father John was dismayed and said that if at any time I wished to return, now or in the future, he would gladly employ me again. I assured him that I would always bear his kind thought in mind and repeated what I had written to the prior, that I would remain on as cook-housekeeper until Mrs Chubb had settled in.

I received three replies to my advertisement. At my request, the prior asked Father John to type me a reference. Now I had three references: one from the gynaecologist, which was hardly of consequence anymore, one from Mr Shagall, and the latest, from Father John, which was simple and conventional.

I eagerly scanned the three replies to my advertisements again. Father John had said I could use the monastery phone at any time, free of charge. The first letter was from a Scot. It was obviously written impulsively and was from an angry man. To paraphrase, he said that he had made up his mind, whether 'she' liked it or not, and that certain other relations could go to –. He wanted a housekeeper, and a housekeeper he would have; he would not make a 'premature' marriage to suit 'them'. Finally, he asked me up to Scotland (on the overnight express) to see his farm. He said he would refund the fare, and if I liked him and the place, and if he liked me, that I could stay on there, in Scotland, as his housekeeper. It sounded like a very precarious position to me. I had no intention of travelling hundreds of miles to Scotland, nor of answering his letter. It was ridiculous and I burned it. Scotland indeed!

The second letter was from a Mr Khan. I arranged an interview with him for 11 a.m. that Saturday. Then I read the third reply, which was from a retired doctor in East London, DoctorSilhou. He had a grown-up family, he stated, all married except his daughter, who up to this point had been housekeeping for him. Now she was going to Swansea University to study medicine and he needed a housekeeper. He was a widower, his wife had been killed in the Blitz and he lived alone. His married son also practised medicine in his surgery, but he lived nearby in his own house and came each morning to his father's surgery to see his patients. I made an appointment to see him on the Saturday afternoon.

Two Interviews

My first interview was in north London with Mr Khan. I dressed in my new coat, shoes and bag, and set out briskly. I had jotted down Mr Khan's address on a memo pad by the monastery phone and had put the paper carefully in my handbag. I arrived early, and Mr Khan was at home but temporarily engaged. A precocious little girl told me to wait. The door to the next room was open and I could hear children talking about their mother and about their father's new love. Finally, Mr Khan was free to see me. An attractive blonde was with him in the sitting-room and he introduced her as Miss Candle, obviously a false name. From the rapport between them I guessed she was already his mistress. I had misunderstood his name on the phone and I had forgotten to bring the letter. On the phone it had sounded like Mr Clan.

'I am Hanna Greally, Mr Clan,' I said.

Here, Miss Candle interrupted. 'No, my dear. It is Mr Khan.' She spelt it out K – H – A – N.

Mr Khan himself stood in front of the fireplace, legs apart like Napoleon, for he was not tall of stature, but stocky. He was a film producer, handsome and oozing power. I had read some months previously a history of Genghis Khan. Nobody had used the horse in battle before him, and that is how he was able to conquer Europe.

Impulsively, I said – 'Are you related to Genghis Khan?'

'Who is he?' he said.

'He was a great man,' I said enthusiastically. 'He tamed the horse, used sheepskin saddles and conquered Europe.'

'I didn't know that,' he said.

His mistress clearly did not like me.

'We will let you know, isn't that right, darling?' she said.

He nodded briefly, completely mesmerised. I never expected to hear from them again and I was right.

Next I set out for east London for my second interview of the day. I hoped that I would be accepted by Doctor Silhou as his cook-housekeeper before evening. The appointment was for 3 p.m. so I had time to have lunch at a café and tidy myself up. Afterwards, feeling refreshed, I hastened to my appointment.

I ascended the twelve steps to the front door of Doctor Silhou's house and rang the bell. Penelope, the daily char, opened the door. Penelope was a typical Mrs Mop. She was married, spoke with a loud Cockney accent, and judged her neighbours by the condition of their front-door steps or porch. If they scrubbed those places daily, on hands and knees with soap and washing soda, then they were all right. If they did not, they were not to be trusted. Penelope considered me, smiling faintly. When I told her my name and I said I had an appointment for 3 p.m. with Doctor Silhou senior, she ushered me into a large sitting-room and asked me to take a seat. She went to tell him I had arrived and I looked round the room while I waited. There was a television on its stand. A bright fire was glowing in a heavy, red, smokeless-fuel heater, and the room was warm and comfortable. Some japonica shrubs in brass pots were in two corners. The rugs, carpets and chairs were old and worn. The furniture was practical: piano, desk, couches. The armchairs had cream and floral covers. It was a very old-fashioned house, but it had character.

Doctor Silhou came in noiselessly. He was always very quiet. He was quite elderly, had a short grey pointed beard and thinning grey hair, and behaved with rather a ceremonious daintiness. He was thin and correct, his suit was dark and respectable, his snow-white collar was starched stiff. When he came to me he smiled, just a ghost of a smile. When the introductions were over I produced my references and gave them to him to read. He read Mr Shagall's reference first and I saw him smile faintly. I wished, silently, that Mr Shagall had not stressed unnecessary details about my sobriety and ability to cook all his favourite Irish recipes.

Doctor Silhou handed me back Mr Shagall's reference and said, 'You cook only Irish dishes?'

'Irish stew, of course, Doctor, if you desire it, but I have some experience of continental cookery.'

I added that I was very good at curries and soufflés, but he did not seem to be interested in those. Next, he read the gynaecologist's reference, and I was relieved to see that he did not make a note of her phone number. Finally, he read Father John's reference from the monastery.

'He says you are sober, and a good Christian.'

I blushed when I thought of those references. All of them stressed my sobriety. You would imagine that I had 'a tendency' or that I did not know when to stop. Then he discussed wages. Finally, he said he would like to introduce me to his son Ferdinand, Doctor Silhou junior, and his daughter Mary. He enquired if I could come to work for him before the first of the next month and I agreed.

He said he knew the monastery well, that his grandsons were pupils at the school, and that he would personally call for me there towards the end of the month. I knew then that I was accepted. I agreed to his suggestion, as now I had at least three cases and taxis were very expensive. Now all I had to do was return to the monastery for a week or so and await Doctor Silhou's arrival. When I left he asked me to give Father John his regards and also Father Prior. I promised I would, and in very good humour I returned home.

Father John was helping two dailies serve the evening dinner when I got back. One of the dailies put a dinner for me on the table in the kitchen and while I ate I told Father John about the interviews. I did not mention Mr Khan, except to say that one of the interviews was not successful, but when I told him about Doctor Silhou he was pleased, and very pleased when he heard he was an old boy of their school. Later that evening in my apartment I wrote to my Uncle Pete and said that I had obtained a new post as cook-housekeeper to a doctor. I did not expect a reply but I promised to call to see him as soon as I was free to do so. (The last time I called he had become upset. I had simply asked him would he take me to the Chinatown I had read about, in some place called Soho, and he was rather rude, replying, 'Certainly not. Do you want me to have my throat cut?' I looked at his throat and secretly wondered who would be bothered.) Now I posted the letter to him in the pillar box outside the monastery; also a letter to Doctor Silhou confirming our arrangement that he would collect me by car from the monastery on the last day of the month.

It was peaceful in my apartment and I wondered was it here my happiness lay, in the uneventful toil and the calm reward of evensong? But I realised that to me happiness was in the seeking, and perhaps the sharing. There was healing of the soul for me here in the monastery, but the body suffered. I seemed to have less time than ever for prayer now. As a busy cook-housekeeper among so many saints, I felt a regular Martha. I wondered would I be happy in the East End with Doctor Silhou?

Dr Silhou

The last day of the month dawned, a pearly sky overhead, birds twittering their finale to spring courtships and adieu to me, I imagined, for this was the day I was leaving in quest of happiness. I had my last lunch at the monastery. I had said my goodbyes to Father John, the dailies and houseboys and to four or five dispensations. At 3 o'clock sharp Dr Silhou drove up the monastery drive to my quarters. I stood waiting with my cases at the door, sad to be leaving yet confidently cheering myself with the thought that it was all for luck.

Dr Silhou pointed out shops and buildings of interest in the East End as we motored along. I did not know anything much about the East End then, but I got to know it later. Lots of good honest people live there, but it was, and is, infamous as a refuge for jewel thieves, burglars, racketeers and other members of the criminal underworld. It was the area of the old opium dens, which are now extinct, and a terrible character called Jack-the-Ripper had frequented it, often with dire results. Dr Silhou's house, which was called the 'Hammer and Anvil', was at the end of the road infamous for the sordid parcel containing a human kidney that Jack-the-Ripper had once posted to a resident there, with the warning that he was on his way. This was close to Lime Street and about a fifteen-minute walk from the docks. As we drove I learned that Dr Silhou was aged seventy, was of Japanese extraction, a natu-ralised British citizen, and was extremely conservative. Funnily enough, his son Ferdinand was not conventional or conserva-tive at all, and even voted Labour.

Dr Ferdinand was very popular with the East Enders, I noticed. I expect he removed lots of bullets from gang members and healed gunshot wounds, for most of the under-world were on his NHS list and squad cars and police were continually parked around the place in alleys and cul-de-sacs awaiting their man. The women absolutely adored him, too, and brought him gifts to the surgery in token of their regard. I did not like some of these gifts, for I had to cook them. One day Dr Ferdinand brought me a plastic bucket.

'Will you do something with this, Hanna? Cook it for Father or something.'

I looked into the bucket. Water was in it and a moving grey shell-like thing.

'What is it?' I asked nervously.

'A live crab,' he said gloomily.

'They know I like fish, but I never meant shellfish or crabs.'

I felt ghastly. I also did not know what to do with a live crustacean.

'Please return it,' I pleaded. 'There is no way of cooking it here,' I said in desperation. 'The saucepans are too small.'

He picked up the bucket wearily and said, 'Just as I thought, Hanna – useless.' Then he returned wearily to his everlasting interviews with the underworld.

Ferdinand was too soft; they played hell with him, he told me once at tea. We were alone as Dr Silhou senior had gone out on a visit.

'Who plays hell with you, Ferdinand?' I asked. (He hated to be called 'Doctor'. I had had to promise to call him Ferdinand.)

'The women,' he answered. 'There am I, at night at home, walking the floor with the baby, trying not to disturb my wife, when the phone rings – at 2 a.m., Hanna, 2 a.m. I expect an emergency – and what do you think it is, Hanna? Women,' he said bitterly.

Life was very hard there for all of us. My duties were onerous and time-consuming. Here is an extract from my diary describing a typical day's routine for me when there were no visitors or any unexpected problems to sort out:

I rose at 6.30 a.m., dressed and made my bed and tidied my room. Opened the window, and said my prayers. I descended to the landing below. I stopped outside Dr Silhou's bedroom and collected his shoes from outside his bedroom door. I left them in the lumber room to be cleaned later, by me. Next I go into the sitting-room, draw back the curtains, open the window, rake the fire, fill it with smokeless fuel, and use the small ash Hoover to clean the fire tiles. Next I take the coal cylinder outside. I go through the French window to the fuel-shed and I refill the cylinder. Next I empty the ashes into the back garden bin, and unlock the back gate, for the convenience of Penelope, the daily, who comes early to clean and tidy the surgery and the patients' waiting-room. I dust and polish the sitting-room before I go back into the lumber room, where I polish Dr Silhou's shoes. I leave them outside his door. Then I lift up the phone and ask the operator to restore normal service. When the phone rings I go down to the kitchen and dining-room. Crake the dog greets me from her basket and I open the kitchen door and let her out to the garden. Penelope knocks and I open the door and greet her cheerfully. I wash my hands and prepare breakfast. I cook rasher and egg for two. I take the milk from the Frigidaire for the jug and heat some of it for the coffee. I prepare a fresh grapefruit, which I decorate with castor sugar and place on the dining-room table. I put on the percolator with the measure of coffee. I make the toast and finish laying the table. If the phone or door-bell rings, I answer each, while awaiting the punctual arrival of Dr Silhou. The postman usually rings then, because of medical boxes, etc. I answer and return to the breakfast table to await Dr Silhou. He comes in at 8 a.m. After breakfast, I recommence housework. I water the flowers in the hall first and remove any faded ones. If all are withered, I take the vases down to the kitchen to clean and prepare for fresh flowers. These I buy from the greengrocer and flower shop combined, opposite, in the afternoon. I Hoover all the carpets and make Dr Silhou's bed. I remove his linen to the kitchen, wash and wring, and hang it out to dry. Next I phone the grocer for supplies and prepare the table and vegetables for lunch. At 10.30 a.m. I prepare the coffee tray for the two doctors and myself. Then I go to the shops for meat and perishables. I return and store purchases. Then I heat the oven and put the joint in for a four-course lunch at 1 p.m. I wash the coffee cups, cook the greens. Finally I put the rhubarb or apple pie into the oven. Have lunch with the doctors. Discussions between them about National Health, etc. Lunch over, wash up. Collect clothes off line and iron, 3.30 p.m. Rake (again) sitting-room fire and refill fuel cylinder. Prepare tea for four, or five if Mary, Dr Silhou's daughter, is at home. After tea take Crake for a walk in the park. Return, prepare dinner. If Dr Silhou is out, leave milk and sandwiches in his room. If alone, take down messages on memo pad for Ferdinand until 11 p.m. Operator changes phone then to Ferdinand's home.

Well, that was one typical day at Dr Silhou's. I usually retired at 11 p.m. after a fifteen-hour day. Although I often felt too tired at 11 p.m. to take a bath, I usually did.

I lost my keys once, and they were never returned. When I was on the way back from Mass, a youth with red hair stopped me on the footpath and asked me for a shilling for a cup of tea. He walked beside me, telling me his hard-luck story. He said he had lost his job. When I arrived back at the 'Hammer and Anvil', I found that my pocket had been picked and my keys were missing. I was furious. I retraced my steps, thinking I might find the youth or the keys. I stopped beside a pub near where the youth had stopped me and saw him outside the pub with three dreadful-looking men. They were swarthy, or grimy, and they had long scars and fresh cuts on their faces. I was scared, but I ignored them and spoke directly to him.

'Have you my keys?' I asked. The red-headed youth pretended he did not recognise me, and the three men leered insolently at me. I knew intuitively that these men had no conscience, so I said cautiously, 'I will give a reward to whoever returns them to me.' Still no response. so I wrote my name and address on a slip of paper and handed it to the red-haired youth, saying 'Take this address. There is a reward, if you should find them.' Then I walked away, miserable and powerless to do anything else, but I felt sure he had my keys. One of the thugs called out after me to forget it and come and have a drink, but I walked on. It was very inconvenient losing those keys, but worse could have happened, I suppose.

I stayed at Dr Silhou's for a year and then I resigned because my Uncle Pete was himself in need of a housekeeper. Of course this was not true, but that was the reason I gave in my note of resignation with the usual excuse, 'for personal reasons'. Mary was back from college by then, so I left her in charge of the housekeeping at the 'Hammer and Anvil'.

When I left Dr Silhou, I obtained my next post by *answering* an advertisement placed by a canon in one of the Church papers. His church was in north London, where he was assisted by two curates in his parochial duties. He also employed a handyman-cum-gardener-cum everything. The canon also owned a huge grey tabby cat called Missal, of whom he was very fond and for whom he provided a tin of cat food every day. I gave her numerous saucers of milk for her delectation. One of my chief duties was to open the tin each morning, divide the contents in two and give her one half at breakfast time and the second half for her evening meal. The canon also liked his food, preferring old-time conventional four-course lunches and late dinners. He was not faddy. He liked baked rice, roast beef and Yorkshire pudding, leg of lamb, cheeses. In fact, the dishes he enjoyed were much the same as his predecessors would have eaten in medieval times. Meal times were irregular, due to church duties (except Missal's of course). One Friday I served Devon sole with lemon to the canon and curates in their dining-room. I was to have fish also, but as I did not like Devon sole, I opened a small tin of salmon for myself and I left it on a dinner plate on the table in my own sitting-room. I served the coffee, cheese and biscuits to the priests, then I returned to my own meal with a bowl of salad in my hand. When I came back into the sitting-room I could not believe my eyes: there was Missal the tabby sprawled across the table, her two paws on my dinner plate, eating my salmon with obvious relish. I told the canon of her misbehaviour. He listened and said gravely, 'You put temptation in her way, Hanna.' Now you know. If you have cats in the house, when serving fish or meat always use a silver dish-cover or similar. Those covers seem to have gone out of fashion nowadays, but, believe you me, they are indispensable.

I stayed with the canon and curates for just one month. When I started there I had agreed to take only one day off. I took the canon's word literally and did not work the day off, but when he asked to see me I was not surprised, for I knew he had something on his mind and I was certain it would not be to my advantage. He said his last housekeeper had never taken a day off and would I mind working for four hours on my day off, just to 11 a.m. I did mind, but all I said was, 'It is inconvenient, Canon, as sometimes I make plans in advance to travel early. I will let you know.' He was obviously astonished at my answer. Following this I wrote the letter of resignation, yet again 'for personal reasons'. I was tired and weary of all these posts, and no holidays, but still I went on to my next position. It was a change of scenery, at least.

The Orderly

My next position was as an orderly in a general hospital in London. I applied for the position despite having no idea what an orderly was or what duties or skills were involved. I included copies of my references with my letter of application. I had an extra reference now – Dr Silhou's. His reference was more refined than the others. He stated that I had also acted as telephonist and receptionist in connection with his son's practice and he stressed the fact that I had been 'very proficient in this sphere'. Naturally, he paid tribute to my cooking and housekeeping ability and it was entirely due to this elegant reference, and my connections with the doctors concerned, that I was accepted by the matron.

The bed-sitter I moved into near the hospital was very tiny and box-like. It was just a bedroom really and a very small one at that. There was no window, as it was just one room of many along corridors. There was no kitchen, just one gas ring, one meter, an iron and one bathroom on each floor. One had to wait or do without. The absence of a window was the worst problem, although there was a fanlight above the door which could be opened. The gas fire would not light sometimes, even when I had just put a shilling in the meter, so I bought a cheap electric fire at a local shop for 27s 6d and plugged that in. The bathroom with a shower was next door to me and at least fifty persons availed of it. When I wanted a bath, I ran inside as soon as the last person left, bolted the door, stripped by the bath, bathed and refused to answer when people asked if I'd be coming out soon. There was a toilet inside the bathroom also and when latecomers at night or in the early hours flushed it, it woke me from my sleep.

To return to my orderly application, I thought that this would be an opportunity to see a hospital again. When I was a probationer nurse in my teens there were no orderlies. I was at that time nurse, probationer and orderly all in one, but the two years I had spent nursing then were of no help to me now, for now I was simply half domestic and half messenger. One of the messages I ran was taking blood samples to the Blood Transfusion block. I was like a vampire hastening from the donor to the laboratory with tiny little sample bottles of blood for testing.

The matron explained that I would also be assisting the nurses by freeing them from some of the more tedious chores, thus allowing them more time to attend to practical nursing. I would give the patients their drinks, and meals, serve elevenses, arrange flowers and put them outside the ward at night, take forms from ward to ward, serve afternoon tea, give out washing bowls if needed and so on. In short, I was to make myself generally useful. My wages were £10 per week but almost £2 was deducted for stamps. The bed-sitter cost £3, so I was no better off financially, but at least I could call my soul my own, and I determined to give it a try.

I commenced my duties as orderly at 7.30 a.m. one Monday morning. I wore a uniform and cap, similar to the nursing uniform. My fellow orderlies were from every nation under the sun. The one I liked best was an Austrian. She could not speak English and her quiet attempts to communicate were amusing and endearing. I worked with her on the Children's Ward, which was enjoyable, for we had a children's party there almost every day. We served the children ice-cream and jelly for their birthdays. We listened to their stories and told them stories and rhymes. Toys were provided – rocking-horses, pedal cycles, teddies, dolls, the lot. The children were curious and lively, easily pleased, and in some wards were just convalescing after a tonsillectomy or other childhood ailment. They recovered quickly and were usually good fun. There were sad cases in some wards, but they received first-class care and attention. The nurses, I noticed, were especially fond of children.

The next week I was put on the Male Wards. A boxer who was a patient there was very nice and courteous to me. Whenever I came to work on his ward, he used to jump out of bed and help me with my duties. The men laughed and joked with him about his sudden spurts of energy. Men, I found out, at least in the wards, hate ventilation; even in summer they prefer their windows closed. Others disliked aerosols, which it was my duty to use occasionally to sweeten and freshen the air.

The following week I was changed to the Women's Medical Ward, where I had to take the right food plate to the right person. The sister in charge, serving all the food from a large mobile electric hotplate positioned in the centre of the ward, constantly consulted her diet chart, was assisted by an orderly. The women on that ward were nice to me also. They were active and cheerful and helped me with the wash-bowls, water and flowers.

A month later I was sent to the Cardiac Wards. Everybody was very quiet there. The nurses wore white canvas rubber-soled shoes or plimsolls. I expect it was necessary – for example when the doctor used his stethoscope to listen to someone's heart. After heart operations, the theatre nurses would leave me with a large stack of white canvas plimsolls to clean. I did this with white canvas cleaner and applicator in the sluice room. It reminded me of the Blanco I had used as a child to clean my own canvas shoes.

A Day Off

Once on my day off, and as I was in London, I decided to visit the House of Commons. I wanted to see the famous building of course, but I went there principally to enquire if and where I could find the maiden speech of my late cousin Michael Reddy, MP. He was an Irish Nationalist Member of Parliament for County Roscommon from 1903 to 1911.

I took a bus and arrived at Westminster in about twenty minutes. About thirty people were queuing outside the House of Commons waiting for seats in the Public Gallery. I took my place at the end of it and it was a good hour, I am sure, before I walked in through the door. I went over to an enquiry office and asked the man there where I could get a copy of my cousin's maiden speech. The gentleman was most kind and advised me to go to The Records Library, where I could examine the relevant volume of Hansard. I decided that, as the day was too far advanced for another excursion, I would proceed to the Public Gallery and listen to one of the debates. So I joined another queue of people, sitting down this time, beneath gigantic statues of ancient warriors, philosophers and modern politicians. A man passed within a yard of me, a strange-looking fellow wearing knee-length fine black stockings with large silver buckles on his patent shoes. He was very imposing, looking neither right nor left as he strode into the chamber marked 'Members Only'.

Many famous politicians passed by. I recognised Mr Heath and Jo Grimond. Soon I was head of the queue and when an usher said 'Next' I was inside. The Gallery was packed with visitors and it was very hot in there. The MPs were talking down below in the arena. They all appeared to be lethargic from the heat. Some were in their shirtsleeves, others had removed their ties. Enervated, they droned on and many yawned and seemed anxious to leave, I thought. I listened intently and was amazed to discover that the subject of their droning was one-way traffic! I had not the foggiest idea what it was all about. It was difficult to hear and there was no excitement at all, so I decided to leave.

I returned to the hospital to work next day and I was sent then to the Male Geriatric Ward. It was very quiet there, as most of the men were outside on the green verge, sunning themselves, reading newspapers or listening to transistors with hearing aids or earphones. Some were playing cards. I spent five quiet uneventful days there doing my usual duties.

On my next day off I decided to try again to find Cousin Mike's maiden speech. With this objective in view I set out for my postponed date with Hansard. I found the huge old multi-storied building, walked up the stone steps to the entrance, and went to Enquiries, where I explained to a girl there what I required. She looked up her Records Book, then directed me to a corner of the room where there was a ceiling-high bookcase of huge plank shelves. She said I would find all of Cousin Mike's speeches there. She gave me paper and a pencil and instructed me to select the passages I wanted from the Hansard volume and write down the number of the page and the column number of the lines I had selected. Then, having completed my 'research', I should hand her back the paper. She concluded by saying she would then order photostat copies of my requirements and post them to me within a week. I thanked her for explaining the system, went over to the book shelves and took down the volumes of Hansard from 1903 to 1911. The speeches were alphabetically recorded, so I found Michael Reddy's speeches near to John Redmond's.

I spent a very interesting morning there, reading Cousin Mike's speeches and selecting for photostating. As I read and wrote down the numbers, people kept coming and going. Some sat near me with other volumes of Hansard and writing notes. Russians with astrakhan caps came and went; I thought I recognised one or two famous people, but I was not certain.

I could not find Cousin Mike's maiden speech recorded so I returned to the secretary at Enquiries. I asked her if there was a separate volume of Hansard for maiden speeches and was a little disappointed when she said no, for in Ireland, as I understood it, maiden speeches in the Dáil were deemed important and were awaited with anticipation. The speeches I did select from Hansard, though, were interesting. I selected passages about the Assize Court cases – one was about larceny committed by a goat. About a week later the envelope with the photostats of my cousin's speeches arrived in the post. They were a reasonable price, I thought – fifteen shillings.

I spent my last week in the hospital as an orderly on the Maternity Wards. It was my first time on a Maternity Ward, and it was a revelation to me. I never knew before that pregnant women sometimes have strange cravings. One woman in a private room there asked me to get her strawberries and pickles.

'Together?' I asked.

'Oh yes, love, they are my favourite dish at the moment,' she said.

Another expectant lady wanted an assortment of jam, mushrooms and bananas. I was sorry to refuse her, but what could I do? I was warned later to pay no heed to unusual food requests.

My duties were the same on every ward. I delivered water, glasses and bottles. I made hundreds of beds, pre-delivery on the table and post-delivery beds in the wards and private rooms. It was London, remember, with a population of between seven and ten million. Babies were born there every few minutes. There were twins, triplets, black babies, brown babies, white babies and some blue babies in incubators. There were embryos visible to all in half-gallon glass bottles. There were some stillborn babies too. One day, while I was doing a chore in the sluice room, a senior nurse left a little bundle there. She placed it carefully on top of a linen basket. It was like a mini Egyptian mummy. The face and head were covered and the whole form was completely swathed in some type of strong bandage material. The nurse said to me as I went to take the mysterious bundle from her hands, 'Leave it safely by; it is a stillborn baby. Do not disturb it; it will be collected later.' She did not say by whom and I left it untouched. From time to time I looked anxiously across at the sad little bundle. Then I began to wonder about Limbo and baptism. However, just then I was sent on an errand to the Blood Transfusion Block with a tiny bottle of blood to give to the chemist there for classifica- tion and when I returned to the sluice room the poor little bundle had disappeared. I suppose the relatives called for it. I hope so. It would be sad to think it had been sent to a School of Anatomy or some such place for dissection.

This incident decided me. I began to think there was no happiness there, no future for an orderly when she had to witness such sad things. Once again for purely 'personal reasons' I tendered my resignation to the matron. She asked me if I would prefer another ward, suggesting the Geriatric Ward. I assured her that it was for 'personal reasons' I had resigned, and I said that I had been offered a position as cook-housekeeper again, in a country town in Surrey. I added that city life did not agree with me beyond a week or two. Well, it was true really. The windowless, gloomy bed-sitter was a depressing place to return to. I had, I explained to the matron, an offer of a job from a retired doctor of Irish descent. He lived in a small town in Surrey. Again, I looked forward to a new ray of sunshine to light my way to happiness.

Dr Joseph OBE

My next and last position in England was as cook-housekeeper to Dr Joseph OBE of Walton, Surrey. His last housekeeper had retired at the age of eighty. He was getting on himself, as he sometimes said to me, to which I would reply, 'You'll receive the centenary congratulation telegram yet.' He would not answer, but a faint smile would light up his serious intellectual face. He had grey hair when I first met him, and was tall – well over six foot – and extremely thin. He was very abstemious in his habits and did not drink, except for the occasional sherry with me or his visitors, who were rare indeed. He was very modest about his OBE. He told me that during the Great War of 1914–18 his hospital for casualties was just about two miles from the front line in France. He was in the Retreat of Mons. Then he retired, but when the Second World War began in 1939 Whitehall asked him to go back to the laboratory to prepare vaccines for the battle troops. He told me all this very quietly one evening while we were both having tea in his study. He did not mention the OBE, but I understood he was awarded it for this war work which he had taken on in his retirement. He described his visit to Buckingham Palace, how he wore ceremonial dress for the occasion and white chamois gloves. George VI conferred the honours. Dr Joseph had dozens of medals in numerous drawers and cupboards in the house. I tidied a cupboard once where I found his old steel battle helmet and a Sam Browne belt.

Life in Surrey was a different kettle of fish from that of London. While there was gaiety, scandal and excitement for all in the capital, Surrey offered its own charms and pleasures. It was beautiful in summer. There were walnut trees, almond trees, lilac and many others I cannot name. The gardens were well kept. On Sundays the inhabitants of Surrey would spend a restful day enjoying the national pastime, gardening. I was a fifteen-minute walk from the Thames. Occasionally, I went for a walk by the river and I often took with me a bag of stale bread to feed the swans. To go for a walk by the river there on a Sunday was like going to the seaside. It was crowded with adults and with children on rubber rafts and dinghies. Large pleasure boats and yachts passed up and down all day from London to Hampton Court and further. It was five miles to Hampton Court by road and often I cycled there on a Sunday afternoon after I had served Dr Joseph's visitors with tea. Dr Joseph once said to me, 'Hanna, everybody in Walton goes to the river on Sunday.'

Two doves had their nest in a large tree at the bottom of Dr Joseph's garden. They made love all the summer, cooing their very own love songs. The woman who lived next door had an apple tree and gave me apples in the autumn. She was fond of wild birds. She bought coconuts and sawed them in half to hang upside down on the branches of the apple tree. 'For the tits,' she used to say. I placed crumbs on the sills for the robins and in the winter, especially if it was frosty and snowing, I would make a tiny little shelter in the garden and leave dry food under it for the birds.

Nearly every family in Surrey had a dog. The neighbours had dachshunds, beagles, corgis, boxers and poms. A very popular dog was the Alsatian. I went once to see the sheepdog trials in Hyde Park in London when I had an hour to spare before my train was due. In the park a panel of judges was deciding which sheepdog was best at its job. A flock of sheep was there in the field and the dogs obeyed commands to select one, isolate another and so on with amazing skill and intelligence.

Talking of parks, that reminds me of another strange encounter I had in Kensington Gardens on another of my days off. As usual I went to rest and refresh myself in the park while awaiting my train back to Walton. The day was hot and I was tired. Many people were there and a well-dressed man sat down on the seat beside me. He wore a navy nap coat and a trilby hat and looked very respectable compared with most of the men around, who were in their shirtsleeves. To my surprise he addressed me.

'Are you Irish?' he said.

'Yes, how did you know?' I replied.

'Just guessed it. I'm Irish myself.'

'From what part?' I asked.

'Tipperary.'

He did have an odd accent and it could have been from Tipperary, but I was not sure; I could not remember the sound of a Tipperary accent. I stood up, looked at my watch and said, 'Sorry, I must go now. I have a train to catch.'

'May I see you home?' he asked.

'Please don't bother. I'm used to travelling alone.' I observed him closely, then I noticed his navy tie. 'You're not a Tipperary man,' I said.

'Why do you say that?'

'Well then, if you are, why did you choose a tie with the crown and thistle on it? You're a Scot. That's the sign of Scotland,' I added.

He looked confused and I began to walk in the direction of the station.

'Let me walk with you as far as the station anyhow,' he said.

I had no time for arguments. I walked on briskly and he fell into step beside me. When we reached the station I stopped and said, 'I really must say goodbye now. I have my return ticket.'

I hastened to the escalator and in a few minutes I was on the Surrey train. As the train sped on towards Walton I thought with amusement of my dull sexless life and resolved to tell

Uncle Pete on my next visit that, after all, I was attractive to at least one man in London, whether he be a Scot or from Tipperary.

The Milkman and Others

Milkmen come and milkmen go, but the right milkman comes along in his tiny milk motor van eventually. The ideal milkman for a housekeeper of my age group would be a conscientious, punctual man of forty-five to fifty who longs for a wife and home, but, because of financial setbacks, is unable to realise his dream. While I was in Surrey, I knew four milkmen; that is to say, almost a new milkman every year. The first three whistled while they worked but forgot to deliver cream, and even sometimes milk on important occasions. Yet on pay day they always charged you for their omissions. Their intentions were not dishonest, I'll allow, but nevertheless it is sometimes inconvenient to try to explain in the cold at the door that no milk or cream was delivered on Sunday, although you left a note out on Saturday. Then he looks incredulous, while you continue in the same vein, saying that there was no point in phoning the dairy on Sunday as nobody answers. There's always somebody there, he says. Yes, you may know that, but always when one phoned on a Sunday there was no reply, and were it not for the kindness of a neighbour, who happened to have a spare pint in her fridge, it would have been a milkless Sunday. Then he usually fidgets uncomfortably and you still patiently explain that the bill he has just presented you with is null and void and inaccurate, simply because he forgot to deliver on Sunday the milk and cream you ordered on the Saturday. At last it begins to dawn on him that you are right, and he makes the necessary adjustments to the bill and whistles on his way back to his little red van. I had three such carefree youths as milkmen. They were probably in love, which might have accounted for their lack of concentration.

Then Mr Sparks came, my new milkman. He was the ideal milkman for people like me, as he took a personal interest in his customers. He would sometimes come in for a cup of tea while his teenage assistant collected all the empties from the neighbours. He always removed his cap when indoors. It was always a spotless dazzling white and matched his immaculate white coat. He would stand outside, and I would know by his hesitancy that this morning was the morning for his cuppa. Then his charming olde-worlde courteous words: 'Well now, Hanna, that is very nice of you. Sure a cup of tea is just what I need to start the day right.' He always said and did the right thing, leaving no doubt in my mind that I was the *only* person with whom he shared his morning beverage. Not every morning of course, but once or twice a week he would linger and I knew then he had time for a cuppa and a chat.

He was most interesting. He was forty-eight years old and past all the vanities of youth. Like myself, he was a great believer in luck. We both expected to win a premium bond prize every month, and thus realise our dreams. In my dreams I wanted a home of my own in Ireland, and security. He also wanted his own home, as he was an orphan and lived in a boarding house. Like me, he longed for a little dog. He dreamed of all the vegetables and flowers he would grow. He blushed then, and I knew he was too shy to say it – he also longed for a wife. He kept me informed of many things: who from our area was going on holidays, who was leaving the district and who was coming. He advised me always to buy Jersey milk, saying it was the best. I once asked him for buttermilk. He said he had never heard of it, but thought he knew what I meant, and he gave me a pint of cultured milk so that I could make my brown bread. He assured me that many housewives bought it from him just to bake bread.

He also knew about beef. I asked him why the butchers wrote on their beef Scottish, English, frozen. I said I had noticed that the average woman bought Scottish or English and poor people and pensioners usually bought frozen. He said they all preferred English beef really but it was more expensive. The real English patriot bought English, he said, because they thought the royal family ate it.

He was a simple man and we got on well. He promised to visit me when I settled down back in Ireland. When I was leaving he told me to write to him care of the Dairy, and when we said goodbye he said he was lonely and would never forget our cups of tea together and our chats. The postwoman admired him, but when I mentioned it once to him all he said was, 'She doesn't look well in uniform, does she?'

The postwoman, who delivered the post on her bicycle, was very fat, but, in an effort to lose weight, had an active outdoor life. She told me this one morning over a cup of tea. She was then over fourteen stone. She was kind and amusing and she also kept me in touch with local events. For instance, I did not know that Stratford Johns was a Catholic. She said he was. At that time he was the hero of the television series *Softly, Softly*. When he opened a fête at the church I attended, she let me go on the bicycle and see him at 3 o'clock that day. The post-woman always knew what was going on locally. She knew three weeks in advance that the Russian Ballet was coming and she booked seats for the two of us.

I had gone sometimes to the theatre when I was with Dr Silhou in London and occasionally with the Shagalls. The plays I saw in my early exile were *The Ginger Man*, *Juno and the Paycock*, *The Severed Head* and *The Mousetrap*. I went to all the best films in London, but when I became housekeeper-companion to Dr

Joseph I was as quiet and retiring as he, just going for the occasional walk by the river. I cycled occasionally to Hampton Court, usually to sit in the park and see the boat races. I did go once to Windsor Castle by pleasure boat, but I did not go in as I had no time that day. I did go on a conducted tour of the palace at Hampton Court and I was very astonished in one royal bedroom to discover that the tapestry-decorated royal bed would have contained at least eight persons.

As I have mentioned, the postwoman was friendly and kind to me. Once she took me to Bingo. I won £3 that night, but I did not go again as I was worried about leaving Dr Joseph alone for too long, especially since the time he had had a small heart attack. I was scared on that occasion, but I made him comfortable, gave him a spoon of brandy and phoned for the doctor. By the time the doctor arrived he had recovered. The doctor said I had shown great presence of mind to think of the brandy, and he warned Dr Joseph to take care not to exert himself unnecessarily. But dear Dr Joseph used to do extraordinary things for his age. I once went up to London on business and when I returned early I found him on a long lean-to ladder painting the garage. He loved carpentry and painting and repair work. He had a spare room upstairs converted into a workshop where he spent many pleasurable hours. He told me he had always loved carpentry and engineering, but it was his father's wish that he should become a doctor. He was a very dutiful son, I should imagine, and he complied with his father's wishes.

Another friend of mine was the greengrocer. He had been in the Merchant Navy but had saved enough to buy a little greengrocery shop with living accommodation. Sometimes, he would deliver my fruit and vegetables personally and accept a cup of tea by the fire. One day we were alone in his shop and I noticed there were some new potatoes marked very cheap. I was surprised, as early potatoes were usually then two shillings per pound. I bought a large quantity and remarked on the low price. He said they were Egyptian potatoes. I thought of all the unsold cheap potatoes in Ireland and asked him why the importers went so far abroad for them. His explanation was as follows: 'Let's say,' he said, 'A ship goes one way, maybe taking guns to Israel or the Arabs. They deliver the guns and then they take back a load of spuds. They pass through the Suez and maybe Gibraltar and nobody wants them there, right, so they take them back to England where they are sold cheap.'

He also knew all about orchids, and about North and South America. He told me once he had been in Patagonia years before, and that it was said there that giants used to roam those parts. Then he put a question to me that I could not answer. 'Hanna, do you think the giants of the Giant's Causeway had any connection with the giants of Patagonia?'

An ingenious thought but I had to give an ingenuous reply, which was that I couldn't say. He was very nice to me. Often, he would stuff an extra orange or apple into my shopping bag and say, 'Try that one, Hanna. Sweets to the sweet.'

One morning I found a baby hedgehog asleep on the coconut mat outside the kitchen door. I was afraid to touch it, as the quills looked dangerous. I went over to my friend the greengrocer and explained about the hedgehog and asked him what I should do with it. He handed me a pair of industrial gloves to protect my hands and told me to carry the hedgehog down to the bottom of the garden, where it probably had its nest with its parents. He said that hedgehogs loved milk and would drink milk from a saucer. I thanked him and went home and gave the hedgehog the milk and carried it in my gloved hands to the bottom of the garden. Next day I saw a large hedgehog drinking from a saucer of milk I had left out for the baby hedgehog. But for those gloves, I might have got severe injuries to my hands, or there might even have been an abandoned hedgehog during hibernation perhaps. I met some nasty people on my travels, as I have related, but the nice ones, like my greengrocer, made up for all the others.

Two Strange Encounters

While Surrey was peaceful and beautiful, it also had its fair share of the headlines. I had been there a few years with Dr Joseph when the Great Train Robbery hit the headlines of the entire world with stunning force. Three million pounds in notes stolen by a gang of ten men from the Edinburgh to London express captured the imagination of the readers of the national newspapers. Wanted notices and photographs were displayed at subways, police stations and post offices, all offering huge rewards for information about the wanted men. Then Leather-slade farm in Surrey was discovered to be the robbers' hideout and again there were dramatic headlines.

As a matter of fact, I once appeared on the front page of the *Surrey Herald* myself. It was a shock, for I had never been in a newspaper before, and there I was in large black print covering almost half of the front page. The first indication I had was when I passed by the local newsagent in Walton. A sandwich board was on the pavement outside and written on it in huge charcoal-black letters was the headline, 'SURREY HOUSEWIFE FOOLS CON-MEN'. Now, I was not a housewife but a cook-housekeeper and, as for the con men, the two men concerned were, in my opinion, amateurs. I was always of the opinion that con men were supposed to be very clever but . . . Well, this is the real story.

One morning two men, obviously working class, came to the back door of the kitchen. I was frying bacon and egg for

Dr Joseph and myself and he was upstairs in his bedroom, dressing. One of the men was very attractive and spoke with a charming voice. The other was rather rough-looking in wind-breaker and jeans. The handsome one said to the other, 'Leave the bag here and go out and check the mains.' The rough one dropped a dark-brown zipped canvas bag onto the floor. As he left I noticed a bulge in his pocket. The other man had a similar bulge. I watched these inexplicable manoeuvres with one eye on the pan and one eye on them.

The handsome one smiled charmingly and addressed me in a reassuring drawl, and I noticed then how very similar he was to Lawrence of Arabia, or rather to the film star Peter O'Toole, who, in his latest role, was idolised by millions.

'We are testing the water for rust. Would you please turn off the taps and do not flush the lavatories for at least two hours,' he said. I told him I had not noticed any rust in the water and he pointed to the sink tap and told me to turn it on again. I did so and said that the water looked all right to me. He replied, 'It looks all right, but give me a cup please.' He filled the cup from the running tap and then came close to me with it. 'Look, do you see the haze?'

'I don't,' I answered. 'Anyway, water is colourless, tasteless and odourless. Why not take a full bottle with you and have it tested properly, in a laboratory? My employer is not very robust. If there is anything dangerous about the water, I shall not use it. I will ring up the Water Board and find out if it is safe to drink.'

He looked curiously alarmed, although in a lethargic Lawrence of Arabia way, and he was about to reply when the other man returned.

'She says she'll ring the Water Board,' Lawrence said quietly, before turning to me and adding in his most charming manner, 'If you go upstairs to the bathroom and turn on the water, you'll see it there.'

'See what?'

'The haze,' he hissed.

By this time my suspicions were aroused. Haze or no haze, I thought, I may be coshed any minute and Dr Joseph's valuables stolen. So, not turning my back on them, I went to the pan on the cooker, grabbed the large knife and fork from it, did my best to look formidable and said, 'I cannot disturb my employer. He may be in the bath. Don't worry, I'll ring the Water Board and find out if the water is drinkable.' I showed them the door, saying 'I am very busy just now. Good morning, gentlemen.'

They exchanged glances and then Lawrence said, 'We'll call back in an hour.' His companion took up the canvas bag from the floor and they both left.

I immediately rang the Water Board and was told they had not sent any men to that area. They advised me to ring the police for, they said, if crooks were not posing as meter men they were posing as water men. When I told Dr Joseph he also advised me to ring the police, especially as the men had said they would return in an hour. When I rang the police station they were very interested. Apparently, similar incidents had occurred recently in the Walton area and they had not yet apprehended the crooks, who had gained access to houses on this pretext about the water and then filled their canvas bag with valuables when the owner was upstairs in the bathroom at their request. An inspector phoned me back and said he would send along two detectives, and would I please give them the details and a description.

When the two detectives arrived I invited them into the kitchen and gave them coffee and apple pie. I described what had happened and the senior detective asked me to describe the two men. I did, and my rather bizarre description was repeated on the front page of the *Surrey Herald* the following Friday. 'He is the image of Peter O'Toole. You can't mistake him if you follow that. There are posters on the subway walls and all over London of Peter O'Toole as Lawrence of Arabia. There you have an exact description.' I added that he had 'sandy hair and greenish blue-grey eyes'. They jotted all this down.

'What was the other bloke like?'

'Common,' I said.

'Did you notice anything at all unusual about him?' he asked, with pencil poised.

'Well,' I said dubiously, 'he had black curly hair, not wavy but *curly*, just like when you have had your hair permed and wet before being set. Unruly,' I explained. They rose to leave and said that they would have a squad car watching the house in case the crooks returned. If they did manage to 'get through the net' I was to phone the station again. On the way out the detective told me the incident would be in the *Surrey Herald*.

'Why?' I asked.

'If they try it again, people will have a description and be warned.'

And indeed the story was on the front page that same week with the headline 'SURREY HOUSEWIFE FOOLS CON-MEN'. Every word I said was there, all about the cup of water and the haze and about watching out for two men, one like Lawrence of Arabia and the other fellow who forgot to have his hair set after his perm. Now, I never said he had a perm. I said his hair looked like – ah well, least said soonest mended, or so the saying goes.

A very different encounter came about one Sunday morning. I was just sitting down to breakfast when the doorbell rang. Dr Joseph was reading his paper in the study. I opened the door and the callers said they were the Gentle Brethren, a religious society, and that they would like to talk to me. I explained, as I let them in, that I was at breakfast but, if they would like to have a cup of tea with me in the kitchen, we could discuss their problem there. Over tea and biscuits I enquired politely what were the Gentle Brethren and what did they want to see me about. When they spoke of converting me, I had to smile.

'I am already converted,' I said, 'I am a Catholic.'

They said there was no difference between their religion and mine; they believed in the Catholic faith, they continued, and they believed in both the Old and New Testaments and preached the Bible. I told them that I also read the Bible occasionally, and they seemed pleased to know this. As the conversation became more involved I noticed they spoke about Jesus and his brothers as natural brothers, and discussed Our Lady's maternity as natural also. It suddenly struck me that they were talking heresy. Not wishing to appear too dogmatic, as I pitied their heretical errors, I interrupted their remarks gently and said, 'I believe Jesus was the only child of his Mother,' for they had suggested she had other sons. I repeated, 'I am quite certain that Jesus was an only child.'

They agreed that Our Lady gave birth to Jesus, but when they said she had other sons, too, I disagreed and said that Our Lady remained a virgin after the miraculous birth of Christ. I knew then, by their ignorance of my faith, that they were poor misguided heretics.

I stood up, indicating that the conversation was over. They stood up also and warned me that 'only a limited number of Christians were destined to be saved'. They continued to argue on the way out to the door, but I was irritated at their attempts to convert me for I knew that Our Lady had only one child, Christ. I repeated my belief again at the door and I also told them, to impress this true fact on them, 'St Joseph, her husband, was a virgin also, and that fact is recorded historically in the Bible by St Luke, who wrote his own account in his Gospel. Furthermore,' I continued, warming to my subject, 'St Luke was also a physician and a close family friend of Our Lady and St Joseph, so he ought to know. And when he wrote of the physical state of '*intacto*', or virginity, you may rest assured that, as a doctor, he knew what he was talking about.'

I opened the door, and they shook hands with me in a rather limp and defeated manner. I thought this might be due to my adroit defence of my own beliefs and my determination to avoid their wily ways, trying to inveigle me into their pit of errors, for I was convinced that it was heresy they were preaching.

We parted amiably enough. The next time they called I explained to them at the door that my priest had told me to tell them once and for all that I, Hanna, did not need conversion and that if they wanted converts there were plenty of pagans and atheists about. God forgive me for sending semi-heretics to pagans, for that would be a very confusing situation indeed. All in all, though, I felt that I had dealt with these visitors as well as I had done with the con men.

A Sorrowful Ending

I spent six happy years with Dr Joseph. In my last two years I took no holiday, as I did not want to leave him with a domestic replacement, even if I found one, for she would not understand his disabilities and might cause him more suffering because he was very reticent and would not complain. I felt she would not be able to cope with his deafness and failing eyesight, his likes and dislikes of many foods. So I remained happy to be of service to him now that he needed me so much. In return he never let me down. For example, he never forgot my birthday. He would come into the kitchen, hand me an envelope and say, 'Happy Birthday, Hanna.' Later on I would open it and find his usual gift, for he always gave me an envelope at Christmas also. Inside there was always a £5 note. He once gave me an electric hairdryer. I used to buy him slippers and pipes and useful gadgets for his birthday. In my last years there, and knowing him so well, I gave him more practical gifts, often a warm pair of pyjamas for Christmas. One of his complaints was a constant feeling of cold, and he used an electric blanket even in summer. He also used an electric heater in his room, one he had made himself in his workshop. My home was there with him and together we led a contented life.

I had not expected Joseph to die. But then suddenly one day he had to be admitted to hospital. It was only to be for a few weeks, a few x-rays, and then came the shock, the phone call from the hospital three days later – gone, dead. I wept. I felt he must have needed me, tried to find me. When Joseph died, a part of me died, too. The part that survives is the loving woman who disguised her love with loyalty and practical service, part companion, part domestic. My world ended when all the everyday chores and domestic duties were no more.

On a beautiful summer day in June the last post was sounded for Joseph by a bugler in the Benedictine abbey near Reading. Gently, he was lowered into the family grave to lie side by side with his brothers, the general, the admiral and the colonel, and his mother, whom he had loved so dearly. (His father lay in a solitary grave in Dublin.) A small group was gathered there, the Benedictines from the abbey, a few relatives, the funeral director and myself. I stood there, a large bunch of roses and sweet pea in my arms. When the abbot handed me the holy water, I stepped forward to the graveside, knelt and looked down onto the coffin below. I sprinkled holy water into the grave, then gently dropped in the flowers. Therein lay my dearest friend, my noble, lovable, kind, saintly companion of six happy years. My eyes were full of tears. For three days I wept, for all the beauty in the world that was no longer for him or for me.

To Joseph

DO YOU REMEMBER, JOSEPH, WHEN you were dying? I did not know. I nursed you for the three weeks before you went to hospital and I moved your bed into the dining-room, the sunny room. You liked that. I made it identical with your own bedroom above. I bought net curtains to let the sun brighten it. I sat nearby in the sitting-room each night with a blanket in an armchair. I could not sleep unless I knew you were all right. Do you remember, Joseph, how each night I undressed you and tucked you in?

The night they told me you had died I was expecting you back in three weeks, the doctor had said, when the x-rays were over. Joseph, you left me your sword. It was in my heart for three days after you died. Was it the sword you wore to the palace when King George gave you the OBE, when you wore those white kid gloves just for one day only? Remember, Joseph, you gave me both pairs. Did they not fit your long fingers? They are worn now, Joseph.

Do you remember, Joseph, your arm around my shoulders? You towered above me, you were so thin and so aristocratic, even when your shoulders stooped. We walked slowly, morning and night, to your study, back to your bedroom, the last sad walks indoors. I had two fires blazing for you. You loved fires, you always felt so cold. You stumbled sometimes, you began to walk with a sort of shuffle, afraid of falling. I held you close, my arm around your waist, your arm around my shoulder. You were going blind. It broke my heart to see you unable to read. Your little transistor and your hearing-aid were good friends then, Joseph.

Your arm was around my shoulders and I led you to your study and I helped you carefully into your armchair in front of the fire. It was a big effort for you, Joseph, but we managed together. I loved you then, Joseph. Could you see me at all?

The night before you went to hospital, Joseph, I sat by the phone in the armchair in the study. I looked in to see you every half hour. You were smiling quietly and I knew you were listening to music in your head. Was it the echoes of what you used to play before you became deaf? You were almost blind then too, Joseph. I began to love you when you became so helpless. Before this I used to admire your independence, your heroism, the way you did the garden, repaired the clocks. They all stopped, Joseph, when you died. Nobody would understand them like you. You made them. I missed your arm around my shoulders. You did love me, Joseph.

But you loved God best. You never missed your morning or night prayers. When I go to Holy Communion, Joseph, God comes to me. I am used to God. He understands pain above all.

Joseph, do you remember when you were going blind and I put my arm in yours and guided you to the Communion rail? We received Holy Communion together every Sunday. Our taxi man, your chauffeur, will miss us; he never missed a Sunday. We were very close then. Then, as you were getting weaker, we arranged for you to have Viaticum while you were waiting for the private room in the hospital. I wish I had been there with you, Joseph. I was to go on the Sunday. The doctor said to me the morning you went that 'with care' you would be all right. I never knew how you died. It was so unexpected. It was your heart, they said, Joseph.

I could not bear to go back to the house after the funeral. The roses were there, but you were not. My heart nearly broke. You broke my heart, Joseph.

I just want to say I love you and I want to thank you for your care and companionship. Goodbye, dear, tell God I love him.

Last Days in England

When Dr Joseph died I was very distressed and could not face a new employer right away, for I was in need of rest and a holiday. I decided to return to Ireland and look for a house-keeping job there after I had had a holiday. Then I had an offer from Dr Joseph's family. They asked me if I would remain on in the house as caretaker for three months. In his will, made twenty years previously, Dr Joseph had arranged for the house to be sold on his death and for his estate to be equally divided between his two nephews and niece. Negotiations could be carried out, but nothing could be legally transacted until probate was granted. This takes three months and thus the relatives asked me to stay on as caretaker until the house was sold. My duties would be to answer the phone from the property agents and to arrange with them times each day for prospective buyers to view it. I would receive the same pay I had been getting from Dr Joseph and they would give me a housekeeping allowance also. As I was grieving and uncertain, I accepted and decided to go back to Ireland for good in September.

People who wanted to buy the house would come in the

daytime. I made appointments with the property agents in the morning and finished about 7 p.m. at night. The nights were very lonely there. Sometimes, I relived the past when I was with Dr Joseph. His workshop was near my bedroom, and it seemed so empty then. His tools were just where he had left them last. The electric grandfather clock that he had made himself was there. All the clocks had stopped. I prayed often and I read *The Imitation of Christ* frequently. I said hundreds of Rosaries and asked the Mother of God to heal my spirit and comfort me. When a month had passed I wrote to the prior of the abbey where Joseph was buried. I enclosed an offering for Mass and prayers for Joseph. In Ireland we call it the 'Month's Mind'. Day succeeded day, and prospective buyers came and went and presumably made their bids. I shopped as usual. I was allowed housekeeping money as well as my caretaker wages, but I was not interested in food and I got by on sandwiches and snacks. Now that there was only myself to cook for I just 'ate to live'.

Towards the end of August, I booked my passage to Dún Laoghaire. It was the Heysham route at that time. I was glad to hear, through another emigrant, that the *Maud* had been taken out of service and replaced by a more luxurious boat. I booked a first-class single this time, as I was anxious not to add sickness to my sorrow by travelling third class again.

One day the family solicitor arrived to pay me and he returned to me my employment card, which he had stamped during my term as caretaker. He said that in recognition of my services to the late Dr Joseph, the three beneficiaries of his estate had decided to give me a parting gift of £100. He added that Dr Joseph had made his will a long time ago and that they felt if he had had time to add a codicil he would have left me something. Joseph had told me all about his will. I know he felt indebted to his family for their great kindness to him when

he was younger. He was a generous man and w   d
to me, although his only income was his pe
prised about the £100, but I was please   s
unexpected bonus. Then one day the re   ll
together. They thanked me for taking care o
for caretaking and said it would please them   t
another £100 from them as a parting gift. Naturally I accepted;
who wouldn't?

The last week passed quickly. My six suitcases and my
trunk with all my good coats in it were in the hallway three
days before I left. I also had a strongbox containing my own
will. How different it all was from my arrival in England six
years earlier. The relatives arrived about 3 p.m. and we had tea,
sandwiches and cake. I gave them the keys to the house. Sharp
at 4 p.m. there was a knock at the door. It was the taxi driver.
I went out for the last time to the tidily hedged little front
garden while the relatives and the driver were placing my cases
and trunk in the taxi. Before I left the garden I looked back.
The relatives had gone back to the door, smiling and ready to
wave me goodbye, but one dear brave face was not there to bid
me farewell. My eyes wet, I shut the gate quietly on the little
home that I had shared with Joseph for those happy years. I
was on my way back to Ireland, with my small savings and the
hope that there I would find a little home for myself.

When I arrived in Ireland my first task was to search for a
home of my own, and eventually I managed to find my cottage.
I found part-time work as a housekeeper nearby. And I shall
probably write *The Story of My Cottage* in the near future, God
willing. But I shall never forget the home I left behind in
England or the love that went into my dear friend's grave on
that bright June morning.